WILD LIFE

A unique vision of our world

"Richard Jefferies: the first and truest nature conservationist." Matthew Oates

Wild Life

Published in Great Britain by the Richard Jefferies Museum Trust

www.richardjefferies.org

ISBN 978-1-8381300-0-8

Text & design: Mike Pringle.
Victorian contextual information: Liz Howell.

FRONT COVER QUOTE: Matthew Oates - ecologist, nature writer, broadcaster, and former National Trust Specialist for Nature.

Printed by Pulsio Print.
Typeset in Bookman Old Style.

This book has been produced to celebrate the Victorian nature writer, Richard Jefferies, and his love of the natural world all around him. In times when our environment and everything it offers us are in peril, and when politics and social cohesion are fragile, Jefferies' words about flora and fauna, agriculture and the countryside, and our relationship with it all, seem all the more relevant.

Everything in the book has been given freely, including the text, design, photographs and all the time taken to pull it together. All proceeds go to the Richard Jefferies Museum Trust, Registered Charity Number 1148966.

Thanks to everyone who has been involved in or supported the development of the book, particularly Jean Saunders and Andrew Rossabi of the Richard Jefferies Society, for their expert views, plus Sarah Singleton, Caroline Rixon, Halina Bartoszewska and members of the Richard Jefferies Museum team for their invaluable input and support. Special thanks also to Elmar Rubio and all the other photographers and artists – where their images are not captioned credits are given at the back of the book.

Index

N.B. Titles are taken from Jefferies' texts, except Victorian context pages (in italics).

Foreword

Foreword

Thomas Hardy has entered into our communal cinematic imagination. He portrayed the rural world that we wanted to have existed with the full sweep and swoop of the heart and the immensity of fate, all supported by a certification of authenticity from his Wessex base. But if 'Hardyesque' has become a description of a romanticised rural idyll (despite his novels being set at a time of great agricultural decline and hardship) his contemporary Richard Jefferies is rooted firmly in the mud and grind of real rural life – coupled with the transcendent, bejewelled observation of the boy slouching the fields around Swindon, gun under his arm, noticing everything.

I first read Richard Jefferies some 50 years ago when I was a student and immediately recognised a kinship that was personal and visceral. I too had mooched the fields around my Hampshire home with a dog or two in tow, dodging gamekeepers, bewildered by life but entranced by every detail of the countryside. The creatures of this agricultural landscape – the trees and hedgerow plants – all spoke to me too and I was sitting reading in the side streets of a town knowing that the greater reality was somewhere back in those fields and woods. Jefferies spoke to and for me across the hundred years that then divided us.

The fact that he was writing effectively in a suburban garret, churning out hack work, made me love him all the more. The world he wrote about was within him and I recognised it within myself even though it had all but disappeared.

Jefferies loved plants and gardens in the same visceral way that I did too. He wrote about the earth with a kind of tender reverence, and Iden in *Amaryllis at the Fair* was the heroic figure I aspired to, despite (perhaps even because of) his worldly failure. The transcendence of *The Story of My Heart* was something I had experienced – and still do. Hodge, hobbling on a stick down the lane from checking the cattle, was someone I remembered from the late 1950s, born whilst Jefferies was still alive. The magic of Greene Ferne farm was something I longed for (and, 30 years later, came to possess).

Now I am heading towards twice the age that Jefferies was when he died but my admiration for him has never diminished. The changes to agriculture and Jefferies' landscape, even in my lifetime, have been huge and often vandalistic. But reverence for the natural world and the need to acknowledge both its fragility and significance is growing. We are learning that we need that world in all its sublime complexity much more than it needs us. This was Jefferies' subject and it has never been more pertinent to the way that we live.

Monty Don OBE

Monty Don is a broadcaster and writer on horticulture, perhaps best known as lead presenter of the BBC gardening television series Gardeners' World.

Introduction

In His Own Words

In 1879, a book called *Wild Life in a Southern County* was published by Smith, Elder, & Co., London. It was written by a Victorian nature writer called Richard Jefferies (1848–1887) and is given as the earliest example in the Oxford English Dictionary of the phrase *wild life* being used to describe the natural world.[1] Now of course, the phrase has become a single word, and it is everywhere.

When Jefferies chose this simple term he wanted to say something particular about nature, to impart a picture of a new world, of the creatures and plants all around us as he saw them: "nature's children – unrestrained in their wild, free life." The challenge that Jefferies had chosen to take up was to share his view of the world through words. But in the mid-nineteenth century, in the earliest age of mass publication and with little availability of books about nature and the environment, Jefferies was a pioneer. A pioneer writing about ecology. Like all pioneers he had to find the right tools, and if that meant making or adapting them himself, then that's what he did.

Jefferies was born on a small farm in agricultural Wiltshire at a time when everything was changing: new technology and cheap imports dominated progress, and poverty and despair were accepted partners of life on the land. With a troubled and financially-struggling family home, the young Jefferies lived and breathed in the countryside around him. He absorbed every detail of the natural world and the people who worked it, good and bad, and he created

[1] *See pages 86 & 87*

new ways to describe it all. Sadly, Jefferies did not live a long life, dying at just thirty eight from the Victorian 'romantic disease', tuberculosis. But in his too-short years he filled every moment. He was a journalist, an agricultural commentator, and a creative writer; he wrote pamphlets and essays, and articles and novels, including some for children; he dabbled in astronomy, history, politics, spirituality and amateur science. Some of his writing drifts, some of it misses the mark completely, but when he writes about the land he loves, his work is beyond compare. And we have it all, the whole train of thought of a single, flawed person who explored, observed and learned from every aspect of the natural world around him, creating messages that we really need to listen to today.

Richard Jefferies shows us a world where birds, insects and wild flowers existed in numbers that now we can only imagine; he warns us that nature holds no special place for human life and will ultimately win any battle we care to have with it; he reminds us of the incredible depths of wild life living in every hedge and patch of grass; he tells us that the Earth can provide all that we will ever need, if we can only develop the better sides of ourselves, push aside greed and share the abundance; and he extols the life-giving properties of simply being in nature, now.

LEFT: 1925 cast of Margaret Thomas's 1891 marble effigy of Jefferies (in the north transept of Salisbury Cathedral).

BACKGROUND: Wiltshire from the Marlborough Downs.

BACKGROUND: Photograph of Jefferies as a young boy.

Childhood

The Green Country

Richard Jefferies was born in 1848 on a smallholding which he later referred to as Coate Farm, about two miles outside the 'Old Town' of Swindon. Until 1928 this was within the ancient Wiltshire parish of Chiseldon, in the north east of the county, which was almost exclusively agricultural land (with the exception of a brick works) stretched out over undulating clay and chalk of the edge of the North Wessex Downs.

The site was on the edge of the tiny hamlet of Coate, next door to the Sun Inn, and with its small fields butting up against those of the much larger Day House Farm and Coate reservoir. It was about 34.6 acres in total, with several outbuildings and fields evocatively named *The Meadow* and *Home Ground*, and more on the other side of the adjacent Swindon to Marlborough road called *Great Axe* and *Little Axe* after their distinctive shapes.

To the south of the farmstead lay Coate Water, a reservoir created by the damming of Dorcan Brook in 1822, initially as a water source for the Wilts and Berks Canal. The reservoir was perhaps the first major sign of the industrial growth, and its need for housing, that was soon to dominate the area and change local agriculture and the countryside forever. In the 1840s, just a few years before Jefferies was born, Daniel Gooch persuaded Isambard Kingdom Brunel that Swindon was the perfect place for the siting of a major new works for the Great Western Railway and within a decade the town transformed from little more than a country village to an industrial powerhouse.

Nowadays the town is still growing. Although there is still much open, agricultural countryside around the site of Coate Farm, especially to the south, it is increasingly difficult to find a spot which is not overlooked by houses or which does not have a road running through the middle of it. Just beyond the pocket of greenery surrounding Coate Water, which is now a country park and includes a 49.3 hectare Site of Special Scientific Interest (SSSI) because of its wildlife and ecology, the M4 motorway provides a constant soundtrack to the area. Housing has encroached from the original Swindon town and from the growth of surrounding areas such as Broome Manor and Liden. To the east, the area known as Jefferies' Land has all but vanished beneath the Great Western hospital complex and the more recent burgeoning development of Badbury Park.

ABOVE: The house and cottage at Coate Farm, plus a turkey!

RIGHT: Details and map of the homestead that Jefferies called Coate Farm. The house and outbuildings are on the left of the pink section of the map.

BACKGROUND: The agricultural landscape of Wiltshire today.

21

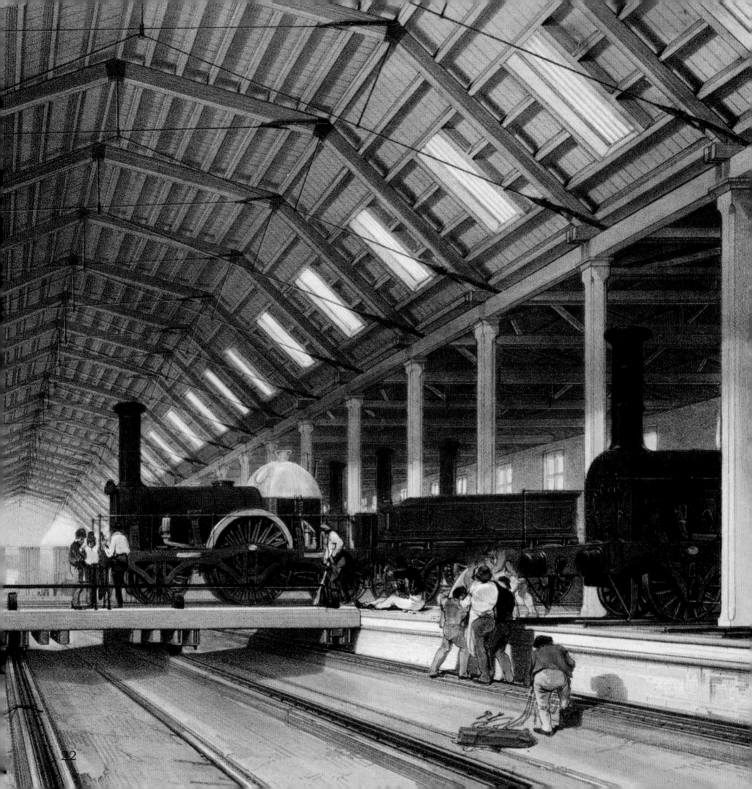

Victorian Swindon

The nineteenth century saw Swindon change from a quiet, country market town with a population measured in the hundreds, to a booming hub of industry, with the arrival of the Wiltshire and Berkshire canal in 1810 and the Great Western Railway (GWR) works in 1842. By 1881 'New Swindon', as it was called, was four times bigger than the original town and had a population of nearly 18,000.

In the 1870's the country as a whole suffered a depression, but Swindon was prospering and the problems affecting other towns did not stop the addition of more rail workshops to the new town, as well as other industries, shops, trades, services and, of course, houses for the growing population. Jefferies, in *A History of Swindon and its Environs*, called the town "the Chicago of the western counties" because of the similarity to the American town in terms of speed of growth.

To keep up with the industrial expansion, everything else developed too: gas lighting was introduced in 1851, spreading to cover the new areas by 1864; a huge corn exchange was built in 1866; a cemetery was founded off Whitworth Road in 1882; recreation grounds and parks were created, including Rodbourne recreation ground in 1889, Town Gardens in 1894, and Cambria Bridge Park in 1899; plus the town became the first place in the UK to have a 'penny' newspaper, with the Swindon Advertiser being established in 1854.

However, despite all this growth, the town was still affected by the limitations of the times, with a general lack of sanitation and poor health. But as understanding grew and scientific advances were made across the country, the town moved forward, with cesspits being replaced by sewers from 1866 and a sewage farm being opened in 1872. In 1853, water from the dirty canals was piped into Swindon houses, but this changed in 1868 when a fresh water supply was created. Diseases like cholera, typhus and smallpox were all present, as they were everywhere, but the new sanitation improved matters, and in 1864 Old and New Swindon elected their first Boards of Health. This determination to look after the wellbeing of local people was furthered by the GWR Medical Fund Hospital on Faringdon Road in 1872, and the creation of the North Wiltshire Victoria Hospital on Okus Road in 1887. Such was the forward-thinking nature of Swindon regarding health that in the mid-twentieth century, Aneurin Bevan, one of the architects of the National Health Service, said of the town "There it was, a complete health service. All we had to do was to expand it to embrace the whole country!"

The motto of the town is, perhaps unsurprisingly, Health & Industry.

All of the Same Name

Although Swindon's new railway industry dominated the area in Jefferies' time, it was agriculture that formed the lifeblood of his family, with a long line of ancestors who were well-off tenant farmers working significant areas of nearby Draycott Foliat in the eighteenth century. Jefferies' great-grandfather, also named Richard Jefferies, purchased the Coate smallholding in 1800, making the transition from tenant to land-owner. But things were to change.

This earlier Richard Jefferies had moved to Swindon in about 1790 after buying the small town's main mill and bakery. As a result of one of his sons, James (known as 'the ghoul of the old mill'), making a mess of running the business, another son, John, was summoned down from London to take over in 1816/17. Despite being successfully employed in the printing business on Fleet Street and not wanting to leave, John turned out to be a very good baker, later adding a grocery business and becoming known as 'Mister Lardy' after his famous lardy cakes. He was also an avid reader with a wonderful collection of books, and a great lover of the countryside, two characteristics that were to pass down to his grandson.

After his father died in 1825, John Jefferies (Richard's grandfather) added a three-storied house to the original cottage at Coate, which he eventually passed on to his son, James Luckett Jefferies (Richard's father), who was born in 1816. James took over the running of the small farm, but not before going to America, where he worked for two years as a labourer along the banks of the Hudson River. He was known to have intense blue eyes, and was more of a thinker than a farmer, who enjoyed spending time tending his gardens much more than trying to run an agricultural business. But his ownership of the farm did not get off to a good start, with a clause in his father's will meaning James had to take out a mortgage of £1,500 to fulfil its requirements. Over the ensuing years this led to him and his wife, Elizabeth Gyde (known as Betsy), drifting into unmanageable debt, meaning that young Richard was born into a family struggling financially, with all the discomfort and insecurity that such a situation would be expected to cause.

ABOVE LEFT: Prayer book with births and deaths recorded on the inside cover. It belonged originally to John Jefferies' mother, Frances Luckett.

BELOW LEFT: Swindon Mill, painted by one of Jefferies' uncles, another John Jefferies.

ABOVE: Jefferies' parents, James Jefferies and Elizabeth Gyde.
LEFT: The Jefferies family christening gown.

"What's your family then, that you should be so grand? You're descended from a lardy-cake!"

Amaryllis at the Fair

"Then, turning to the left, I found some shelter behind the cart-house and stable wall: not so good a strolling place, but better than none. If the breeze shifted south or west, quarters often cold in winter and spring, when the air blows full of moisture, there still remained the 'paving', as it was called: a broad footpath flagged by the house on the north side.

The swallows flew underneath, low down over the surface of the road. High as the great blue doors were, this leafy loophole flanked them. Years ago, it seemed an event when the second door was opened, not without labour, for the passage of the waggon. It had to be heaved off  the central block, swung back, and propped there with the iron bar attached to it. The waggon came rolling in with a load of hay; wisps caught against the ivy; against the eves even; the heavy weight made a deep sound, between the walls; the load, as it passed, shut out the light momentarily from the windows that fronted to the hollow way, and the top rose nearly level on to the roof there above the swallows' nest under the thatch."

The Blue Doors

RIGHT: The farm today, with stables and hayloft in the foreground, original labourer's cottage and newer house in the background, and the cart-house in between.

ABOVE: The same view in the 1950s.

Passions of Childhood

A Victorian childhood in rural Wiltshire was not easy at the best of times, especially with troubled family finances. But life for the two-year-old Jefferies started with tragedy too, as his elder sister, Ellen, was killed by a runaway horse outside the house when she was just five years old. It is hard to imagine the impact that such an event would have had on Jefferies' parents, but certainly their relationship with their next sibling will have changed, and not for the better. The death of Ellen particularly hit Jefferies' mother, Betsy. Having been born and bred in Islington, London, Betsy was already unhappy living in a small, close-knit community in the depths of the countryside. She missed mixing in Victorian society, and was generally nervous and perhaps even neurotic. The loss of her first child, in such terrible circumstances, must have made life unbearable.

Whether it is directly connected or not we shall never know, but not long after Ellen's death, young Richard was sent to stay with his mother's sister, Aunt Ellen (after whom Jefferies' elder sister had been named) and her successful Fleet Street printer husband, Thomas Harrild. Jefferies stayed with the Harrilds in well-to-do Sydenham, Kent until he was nine. Here he attended preparatory school and returned to Swindon only during the summer holidays. It can't have been easy being away from home, but Jefferies developed a strong and loving relationship with Aunt Ellen. Thanks to her he received a strong foundation in formal education, as well as being given a taste of a more 'sophisticated' world outside the rural agricultural life he was from. His formal education continued erratically when he eventually returned home, through small private schools. His parents had a further three children: Henry (1852), Sarah (1853), and Charles (1858).

In 1881 and 1882, Jefferies' childhood in Coate, or perhaps the huge gaps in it, formed the basis for two children's novels with a young main character called Bevis: *Wood Magic: A Fable* (1881) and *Bevis: the Story of a Boy* (1882). The first book is set in the gardens of a farm and the local wood, and the second takes place primarily around a lake. From the similarities between the book settings and Coate, there is no doubt that both tales, although fictionalised, are heavily autobiographical.

Wood Magic is a complex political fantasy. It follows the trials and tribulations of the local fauna and flora, all of which can talk, as war breaks out between Kapchack the evil one-eyed magpie, and Choo Hoo, Emperor of the local pigeon population. The book depicts a child named Bevis who spends almost his entire existence alone in the gardens, where his only real friends are the birds, animals, flowers, trees, insects, fish, as well as the water of the brook and the wind.

Bevis is a more straightforward adventure story, with an older Bevis and his friend Mark (probably based on Jefferies' younger brother, Henry) exploring the excitement and dangers of a lake they call the 'New Sea.' In the book we get a glimpse into the childhood Jefferies spent after his return from Sydenham, with wild swimming, raft making, sailing a boat, fighting mock battles, fishing, and shooting local wild fowl with a gun the boys make themselves. But the background for the story is the natural landscape itself, playing as much of a role as any of the human characters. The book was written around the same time that Mark Twain was writing about the adventures of Tom Sawyer and Huckleberry Finn on the other side of the Atlantic. It has been published in numerous editions, including one version illustrated by *Winnie-the-Pooh* artist, E. H. Shepard.

LEFT PAGE: Jefferies' mother and, below, Aunt Ellen. Plus, child's shoes from the Baden family which Jefferies eventually married into.

ABOVE RIGHT: Jefferies as a young boy.

RIGHT: Taxidermy magpie.

"But no sooner was Bevis released from the dinner-table, than he was down on his knees at his own particular corner cupboard, the one that had been set apart for his toys and things ever since he could walk. It was but a small cupboard, made across the angle of two walls, and with one shelf only, yet it was bottomless, and always contained something new.

There were the last fragments of the great box of wooden bricks, cut and chipped, and notched and splintered by that treasure, his pocket-knife. There was the tin box for the paste, or the worms in moss, when he went fishing. There was the wheel of his old wheelbarrow, long since smashed and numbered with the Noah's arks that have gone the usual way. There was the brazen cylinder of a miniature steam-engine bent out of all shape. There was the hammer-head made specially for him by the blacksmith down in the village, without a handle, for people were tired of putting new handles to it, he broke them so quickly. There was a horse-shoe, and the iron catch of a gate, and besides these a boxwood top, which he could not spin, but which he had payed away half the savings in his money-box for, because he had seen it split the other boys' tops in the road.

In one corner was a brass cannon, the touch-hole blackened by the explosion of gunpowder, and by it the lock of an ancient pistol – the lock only, and neither barrel nor handle. An old hunting-crop, some feathers from pheasants' tails, part of a mole-trap, an old brazen bugle, much battered, a wooden fig-box full of rusty nails, several scraps of deal board and stumps of cedar pencil were heaped together in confusion. But these were not all, nor could any written inventory exhaust the contents, and give a perfect list of all that cupboard held. There was always something new in it: Bevis never went there, but he found something.

With the hunting-crop he followed the harriers and chased the doubling hare; with the cannon he fought battles, such as he saw in the pictures; the bugle, too, sounded the charge (the bailiff sometimes blew it in the garden to please him, and the hollow 'who-oo!' it made echoed over the fields); with the deal boards and the rusty nails, and the hammer-head, he built houses, and even cities. The jagged and splintered wooden bricks, six inches long, were not bricks, but great beams and baulks of timber; the wheel of the wheelbarrow was the centre of many curious pieces of mechanism. He could see these things easily. So he sat down at his cupboard and forgot the lecture instantly; the pout disappeared from his lips as he plunged his hand into the inexhaustible cupboard."

Wood Magic: A Fable

1

Wood-Magic Sir Bevis

Chapter 1. [such was his 'pet' name]

One morning as little "Sir" Bevis
was digging in the farmhouse garden, he saw a
daisy, & throwing aside his spade
sat down on the grass to pick the
flower to pieces. He pulled the [illegible]
tipped petals off one [illegible] things
dropped they were [illegible] he gathered
a bright [illegible] the white juice
[illegible] which drying presently left
[illegible] with brown spots. Then
[illegible] got a bennet from its
sheath & bit & sucked it till his
teeth were green from the sap. Lying at
full length he drummed the earth with his
toes, while the tall grass blades tickled his
cheeks. Presently rolling on his back

BACKGROUND: First page of 'Wood Magic' original manuscript. Young Jefferies' toys, like those of Bevis, were just the things he found around him.

Southwards, looking seawards, instead of the long path of gold which wavelets strew before him, the sun beamed in the water, throwing a stream of light on their faces, not to be looked at any more than the fire which Archimedes cast from his mirrors, melting the ships. All the light of summer fell on the water, from the glowing sky, from the clear air, from the sun. The island floated in light, they stood in light, light was in the shadow of the trees, and under the thick brambles; light was deep down in the water, light surrounded them as a mist might; they could see far up into the illumined sky as down into the water.

The leaves with light under them as well as above became films of transparent green, the delicate branches were delineated with finest camel's hair point, all the grass blades heaped together were apart, and their edges apparent in the thick confusion; every atom of sand upon the shore was sought out by the beams, and given an individual existence amid the inconceivable multitude which the sibyl alone counted. Nothing was lost, not a grain of sand, not the least needle of fir. The light touched all things, and gave them to be. 'Magic,' said Bevis. 'It's magic.' "

Bevis: The Story of a Boy

BACKGROUND: *The reservoir in the country park at Coate Water with its unique concrete diving board. On the horizon is another Jefferies haunt, Liddington Hill.*

33

Victorian Education

Education, like many aspects of life in Victorian England, depended on social class. For the children of the wealthy, education was clearly delineated along gender lines. Initially, both boys and girls would be educated at home, but when they reached around ten well-off boys might go to school, for example, Eton and Harrow, to acquire classical knowledge and sporting prowess before joining the cultured elite of society. Rich girls, on the other hand, were often tutored at home by a governess to prepare them for marriage and womanhood, learning how to conduct themselves appropriately, and picking up skills such as playing the piano or flower arranging, which would be important for married life.

Queen Victoria's own education was unusual in that she was actually encouraged to acquire knowledge by her personal tutors. She read widely and could speak a number of languages, putting her in the unique position, as a woman, of having a superior understanding of world affairs than many of the male prime ministers who served under her.

The middle classes in Victorian times were keen to educate their children, and had the financial means to do so. New public schools were created where middle class boys were taught to emulate the educational achievements of wealthier boys. Richard Jefferies spent a short time at the 'National School' in Swindon. For poor children, anything but the most rudimentary education was out of reach. It was a luxury that working class families, struggling to keep themselves alive, simply could not afford. Children as young as five were either employed, or made to work at home, where families were paid, very poorly, by the quantity of goods produced. Their efforts left them with no time or money for learning.

Near here stood Swindon's first free school, opened circa 1764. In 1836 it was replaced on the same site by the National School, itself closed in 1870 and demolished in 1962.

In the 1830s/40s legislation gradually began to reduce working hours, for example, the 1844 Mines Act banned all women and girls, and boys under ten, from working underground. However, economic needs of the family, which demanded that children became wage earners as soon as possible, still outweighed any desire of a working class parent for their child to be educated. Nonetheless, there were some efforts to educate poor children, driven by philanthropic individuals or churches. 'Ragged' schools taught the poorest children, including orphans and the children of convicts, but the system was rife with exploitation.

As the century progressed there was increasing pressure for universal state-run education and in 1870 the Elementary Education Act was passed, stipulating that all children between the ages of five and ten receive a basic education. Part of the impetus for this change came from industrialists who perceived a need for more educated workers to compete with other industrial nations. The 1870 Act was, however, far from ideal, since it stressed that for girls this basic education was to focus on domestic skills, and most parents still had to pay for their children's education.

Hunter and Explorer

Having left school at fifteen, Jefferies was by all accounts the archetypal teenager: no desire to work, hair too long, no interest in his siblings, wandering alone in the country lanes, shabby clothing, a worry to his parents, and above all a dreamer through and through. When just sixteen, in 1864, he and a cousin, James Cox, ran away with the grand idea of reaching Russia. Unfortunately, no sooner had they crossed the Channel, than the boys' grasp of French proved inadequate and they had to return to England. Undaunted, the adventurers found an advert for cheap crossings from Liverpool to America, so decided to head that way instead. Plans were again foiled when their money ran out and an attempt to pawn their watches alerted the local police, who promptly sent the boys back home again. The two week adventure was over, and Jefferies returned to his lonely country lanes. All of this may all have led to an impression of idleness, a temporary fate suffered by all teenagers, but Jefferies was far from idle.

During these years, in the mid 1860s, the teenage Jefferies was given permission to use part of the farm's attic as his study – a den with a bed and a writing desk among apples, cheeses and long-disused furniture. Here he made endless notes, drawings and observations, worked on articles and books (even writing a 75,000 word novel, *Ben Tubbs*,) wrote countless letters, and read anything he could lay his hands on, from Shakespeare to Byron, and from Scott to Homer.

The trip to Russia may have been a blow-out, but whenever Jefferies wasn't reading or writing in his room, he would spend his time exploring more local haunts, in the countryside around Coate and up on the Marlborough Downs. Much of the time these trips would be driven by a desire to fish or shoot game, skills he'd been learning from his father since he was eight, and later improved upon with the friendship of the gamekeeper on the nearby Burderop estate. In *Bevis*, the writer describes the methodical building of a matchlock gun, all done in secret, giving a glimpse into the world of the younger Jefferies. But hunting was only part of the adventure. All the time Jefferies was outdoors, he was observing the nature around him, learning the names, behaviours and habits of the wildlife, and getting to know the trees, shrubs and flowers. Such was his energy and keenness to absorb the natural world, the young man's walks would sometimes take him as far as Uffington or Savernake Forest, respectively twenty and twenty-five mile round trips, not including the exploration he would do there. And he recorded everything he saw – material for the hundreds of articles, essays, stories and books he would later write.

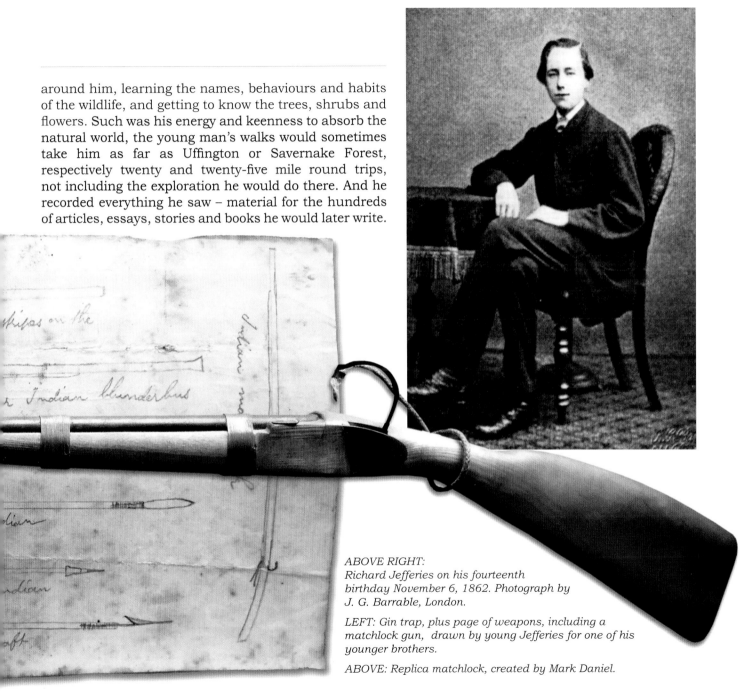

ABOVE RIGHT:
Richard Jefferies on his fourteenth birthday November 6, 1862. Photograph by J. G. Barrable, London.

LEFT: Gin trap, plus page of weapons, including a matchlock gun, drawn by young Jefferies for one of his younger brothers.

ABOVE: Replica matchlock, created by Mark Daniel.

BACKGROUND: Photograph of Jefferies aged 23.

Adulthood

A Change Began

At age sixteen, Jefferies was every bit the chatty, cheeky teenager. In one of his regular letters to Aunt Ellen he tells her about the heat of the summer: "We are burnt up or rather other people are. I'm glad of it. It can't be too hot for me. 90° in shade is nothing here. We look like Portugese or kidney beans." But despite the heat, Jefferies says that swimming has been barred at Coate: "Shabby trick of Dunsford the Canal Superintendant this year – he's stopped bathing at the reservoir. Wish there was no police – we'd duck him." And, like all good teenagers, he can't resist the temptation to ask for financial help: "Wish you'd grease my carriage wheels with a little gold dust. Delicate hint that."

In March 1866, four months after his seventeenth birthday, childhood fun came to an end and Jefferies took up a job at the *North Wilts Herald* newspaper. His duties included reporting, correcting manuscripts and proofs, and reviewing and condensing articles. Outside work, he also pushed on with his own writing ideas. Shortly after he turned 18, the aspiring author was commissioned to write *History of Malmesbury* and, later the same year, *History of Swindon*.

However, the year was tainted by a more serious change, with Jefferies suffering a "bad illness" between July and September. The details of the illness are not known but it is fairly certain that what the young man was experiencing was the start of his lifelong battle with tuberculosis. Perhaps because of this, or perhaps because of family tensions, he took to walking regularly up to the Iron Age hillfort of Liddington Hill. Here, as he reports later in *the Story of My Heart,* he could escape what he describes as "the heaviness accumulated at home", and started to realise that the beauty of the countryside not only filled him with awe, but also with a desire to better understand existence itself: our part, or meaning, in the greater mysteries of the natural world.

RIGHT: Letter to Aunt Ellen, written on 17th August 1864 - "A miserable day."
BACKGROUND: Liddington Hill.

They say it is a very pretty place as far as vicars, trees, rivers, crayfish, eels and small potatoes are concerned. I know nothing more.

There's no news - not a particle.

A printer would go mad, an editor wild. There's absolutely Nothing Doing nor nothing to be done.

All is talking and such talking. Insipid, ridiculous & puerile.

A few stars shot last night but I never heard of any damage having been done.

We are burnt up or rather other people are. I'm glad of it. It can't be too hot for me. 90° in shade is nothing here. We look like Portugese or kidney beans.

I haven't seen a fire since last Christmas - its scandalous. That Clerk of the Weather - wish he'd burn his fingers.

So your sea siding again. Glad to hear of it. Hope you won't drown - Wally can't swim.

As for myself I'm going, going, going but for my life it's a long way. Wish you'd grease my carriage wheels with a little gold dust. Delicate hint that.

Tell Sally I'm glad she's not coming home - there will be some apples to eat this year. That's one comfort. One can get the stomach ache then in a quiet, respectable way.

Uncle Tom comes down Saturdays - does he. Have you got an opera glass but I suppose you'd be too tired to look at the comet. Just below the Pleiades 2 in the morning.

Shabby trick of Dunsford the Canal Superintendent this year - he's stopped bathing at the Reservoir. Wish there was no police - we'd duck him.

Aunt Annie is with you bet a 1£ (if I had it). Just like her. Give her my love and a smack. As for the children - they're loves but Heaven be praised they're out of my hearing.

a bore.

Love by the bushel x x c v c

I am

Myself according to last accounts

R. Jefferies.

Coate
Nr Swindon
Wilts.

Coate
Au 17th '64
A miserable day

...ed this morning
...d arrived and
...st answers it.
...want to know
...individuals
...nant place have
...must read, mark
...arah a letter arrived
...Sunday informing
...was quieter - in
...e medicine - but
...Of course not.
...Its their interest to keep her there as long as possible. She was conveyed there early Wedday nes morning (10th) in custody of Father & Mr Hall in a two horse fly. The 'there' means Fairford. Everybody has heard of that place - an awful wicked place. Even the Church windows are painted with staring figures of imps & other occupants of the Bottomless pit.

41

My heart was dusty, parched for want of the rain of deep feeling; my mind arid and dry, for there is a dust which settles on the heart as well as that which falls on a ledge. It is injurious to the mind as well as to the body to be always in one place and always surrounded by the same circumstances. A species of thick clothing slowly grows about the mind, the pores are choked, little habits become a part of existence, and by degrees the mind is inclosed in a husk. When this began to form I felt eager to escape from it, to throw off the heavy clothing, to drink deeply once more at the fresh foundations of life. An inspiration – a long deep breath of the pure air of thought – could alone give health to the heart.

There is a hill to which I used to resort at such periods. The labour of walking three miles to it, all the while gradually ascending, seemed to clear my blood of the heaviness accumulated at home. On a warm summer day the slow continued rise required continual effort, which carried away the sense of oppression. The familiar everyday scene was soon out of sight; I came to other trees, meadows, and fields; I began to breathe a new air and to have a fresher aspiration. I restrained my soul till reached the sward of the hill; psyche, the soul that longed to be loose. I would write psyche always instead of soul to avoid meanings which have become attached to the word soul, but it is awkward to do so. Clumsy indeed are all words the moment the wooden stage of commonplace life is left. I restrained psyche, my soul, till I reached and put my foot on the grass at the beginning of the green hill itself.

Moving up the sweet short turf, at every step my heart seemed to obtain a wider horizon of feeling; with every inhalation of rich pure air, a deeper desire. The very light of the sun was whiter and more brilliant here. By the time I had reached the summit I had entirely forgotten the petty circumstances and the annoyances of existence. I felt myself, myself. There was an intrenchment on the summit, and going down into the fosse I walked round it slowly to recover breath. On the south-western side there was a spot where the outer bank had partially slipped, leaving a gap. There the view was over a broad plain, beautiful with wheat, and inclosed by a perfect amphitheatre of green hills. Through these hills there was one narrow groove, or pass, southwards, where the white clouds seemed to close in the horizon. Woods hid the scattered hamlets and farmhouses, so that I was quite alone.

I was utterly alone with the sun and the earth.

The Story of My Heart

43

Dignity and Manhood

Jefferies settled into his work as a local newspaper reporter, contributing over the following years not only to the *North Wiltshire Herald*, but also to the *Wilts and Gloucestershire Standard*, and the *Swindon Advertiser*, with the encouragement and support of the latter's editor, a local man named William Morris, who was a fierce champion for animal welfare. But at home, financial worries and unhappiness were slowly eating away at family life. To make matters harder, in July 1868 Jefferies was struck again by serious illness, this time believing, mistakenly, that consumption (as tuberculosis was known) had been avoided. Nonetheless, as he moved in to his twenties, he continued writing on a variety of topics beyond his professional work, driven by a desire to be published by a London publishing house, and putting in the work necessary to make it happen: "People often take horses to twenty markets before they sell them. I mean to take my book to every market I can find – to try every publisher."

Jefferies' also continued writing to his Aunt in Sydenham, and received moral and sometimes financial support in return. At age 21, in 1871, he told her that he was "seriously engaged" to his childhood friend and neighbour, Jessie Baden. But the course of true love did not run entirely smoothly, with objections from one of Jessie's half-brothers actually leading to blood being drawn. Thomas Baden had apparently written a letter which "blackened" the character of Jefferies and an unnamed lady, possibly insinuating that his neighbour was responsible for the pregnancy of a local girl. Jefferies was so incensed that he confronted Thomas, a well-built former Guardsman, and his friend, but came off worse in the scuffle that followed. Undaunted, Jefferies pursued the matter in front of Swindon magistrates, and Thomas was forced to apologise. One can only assume that things settled down after that since Jefferies' engagement to Jessie continued uninterrupted.

It must have been hard for Thomas, a soldier-turned-farmer, to see another young man refuse to follow in his father's farming footsteps, choosing instead a life of rambling, reading and writing. Conversely, it cannot have been easy for Jefferies to ignore the pressures of everyday Victorian agricultural life and pursue his unusual passions.

He was no ordinary young man.

RIGHT ABOVE: The true love of Jefferies' life, and future wife, Jessie Baden.

RIGHT: Gold locket with photograph of Jefferies as a young man.

"I must be different from them,
must be a poppy in a cornfield."

Letter to Aunt Ellen, 1868

45

Writing of Letters

By the early eighteen seventies, Jefferies had fully committed himself to the idea of a life as a professional writer. He was reporting and editing articles for the local newspapers on agricultural matters, political meetings, elections, court proceedings, and market activities, as well as developing something of a passion for researching and recording local history. But this wasn't enough to satisfy the young man's ambitions. Beyond his paid work he had also started a number of novels, and even decided to share his limited writing experiences through his own guide: *Reporting; Editing & Authorship: Practical Hints for Beginners in Literature,* which was published in 1873. However, it was a series of letters to *The Times*, in November 1872, that gave him the break he yearned for.

The letters were about Wiltshire agricultural labourers, but it was not the subject that was the crucial thing about them. As the poet Edward Thomas later describes it, in his introduction to *The Hills and Vales*: "In 1872 he (Jefferies) discovered part of his power almost in its perfection. He wrote several letters to *The Times* about the Wiltshire labourer, and they were lucid, simple, moderate, founded on his own observation, and arranged in a telling, harmonious manner. What he said and thought about the labourers then is of no great importance now, and even in 1872 it was only a journalist's grain in the scale against the labourer's agitation. But it was admirably done. It was clear, easy writing, and a clear, easy writer he was thenceforth to the end."

Publication of the letters raised awareness of Jefferies to other publishers, such as *Fraser's Magazine for Town and Country* and *New Quarterly Magazine*. Before long he was writing articles on a regular basis, all relating to the land and the people who lived on it.

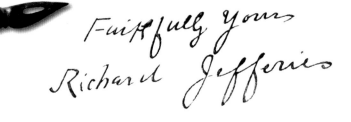

Faithfully yours
Richard Jefferies

Although Edward Thomas dismisses the content of the letters to *The Times* as unimportant, focusing instead on the quality of writing, it is worth noting that Jefferies' reason for submitting them was to defend farmers against what he saw as the ingratitude of their workers. This was to be expected, given his own background as the son of a farmer, and was in keeping with the Conservative values of *The Times*, and magazines like *Frasers'*, but this view would change later.

Importantly, what we see in these letters is the start of a viewpoint about how the land, its people and its produce, are all inextricably linked. Jefferies, the 'country' or 'nature' writer, discovered early on in his career that our relationship with nature is as much about us, the human race, as it is about flora and fauna and sun and stars.

FAR LEFT: Agricultural labourer on Coate Farm.

LEFT: How Jefferies' letters to The Times were reported in the local Western Gazette.

"Sixty years ago the farmers were the ruling class. The towns then had not acquired their present preponderance, and the electors in the country districts, whether for county or borough, were entirely in the landed interest. Perhaps nothing so contributed to their loss of power as the practical introduction of steam and the consequent enormous development of trade. But after half a century indications are not wanting of the inevitable compensation which sooner or later follows human changes. The development of trade and manufacture caused a corresponding increase of population, until at the present moment the demand for bread so largely exceeds the home supply that the imports of foreign corn are enormous in bulk. At first this reduced the political and commercial status of the farmer still lower; his produce was driven out of the market by vast consignments from abroad. But with the demand for corn came a still larger – a disproportionately larger – demand for meat. Corn could be imported, meat could not (at least not in appreciable quantities or quality), and the immediate result, as soon as this was felt, was a rise in the prosperity and importance of the farmer. His attention was at once turned to the production of meat. The cattle, it is true, were not actually fed on the corn which should be human food, but in effect they were, since the vegetables and products upon which they were fatted were either manufactured from or took up the room of such food, thus still further reducing the real – though not, perhaps, the apparent – supply of English corn. Gradually, in fact, England is becoming a meat-producing country as opposed to cereal crops, and the land is turned into vast fatting stalls for the city markets."

From 'Future of Farming', Jefferies' fourth letter to The Times, 15th October 1873.

P. Blanchard.

Victorian Publishing

Like many things in the Industrial Revolution, printing and publishing made huge leaps forward in terms of volume and quality. The industry took full advantage of people moving into the cities, increasing both workforce and customer numbers; there was increasingly efficient movement of raw materials and finished publications, as the railway network and the regularity of its services grew; and technology saw ever faster, bigger and better printing presses and other necessary equipment.

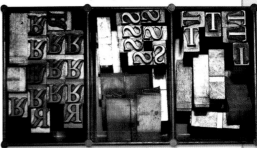

Nonetheless, printing in the nineteenth century was not like the multi-million-copy computerised systems of today. Rather, it was dominated by hand processes, as of course was writing itself. Before a book reached its readers it first had to be written, in pen on paper, before being passed onto a compositor who would 'set' the whole text in metal trays using countless individual letters, each made in reverse, out of lead. When all the pages were set, a proof copy would be printed and sent to be checked, with fines being imposed on the compositor for any mistakes found. Only when everyone – publisher, editor, author and printer – was happy with the text would the pages be fixed into the presses ready for printing. Originally presses too were hand operated, with each page being 'pressed' individually, but by the mid-nineteenth century machinery had improved, with 'relief' and 'intaglio' presses able to turn out copies by the thousands. The loose sheets would then be cut down to the right page size before being sent to a bookbinder to have a cover attached.

Because of the time and money that printing required, publishing itself was often done a bit at a time, with serialised stories or individual essays being published in periodicals or newspapers, before being sold collectively as a book. This ensured that there was a readership before costs became too high.

As well as his relationships with publishers as an author, Jefferies had a few family connections too. His grandfather, John, before he returned to take over the running of the family farm, worked in London for Richard Taylor & Co., a leading printer of natural history and scientific works. One of Jefferies' uncles, Fred Gyde, was a freelance wood-engraver who also worked for Taylor, and Charles Gyde, Jefferies' maternal grandfather, was manager and chief binder at the company. Also, the husband of Jefferies' aunt, Ellen, was Thomas Harrild, a letterpress printer in Shoe Lane, London, and brother of Robert Harrild of Harrild & Son, internationally famous as makers of printing presses and machinery. However, while Jefferies' career as a writer may have been influenced by these links, it did not automatically give him access to being published. Being published in Victorian times was no easier than at any other time and all authors, Jefferies included, had to submit and re-submit their work to publishers, and live with the inevitable rejection letters.

BACKGROUND: *Photograph of Jefferies as a smart young professional.*

Agriculture

Years of Agriculture

HERE LIVED
RICHARD JEFFERIES
1875 - 1877

Cirencester
Civic Society

74 Dyer Street

1904. Architect:V A Lawson. The
Wiltshire & Gloucestershire Standard
newspaper was founded in 1837.
Richard Jefferies, the Wiltshire
author, was at one time its
chief reporter

As he progressed into his twenties, Jefferies grew into his profession, establishing himself as a respected journalist, particularly in matters relating to agriculture where his experience and observations of farming life and nature-rich rural settings gave him an authentic and knowledgeable voice. The work kept coming in, with him becoming chief reporter at the *Wilts and Gloucestershire Standard,* based in nearby Cirencester. This was in the late 1860s and early 1870s, at a time dubbed 'The Golden Age' of arable farming, the perfect time for a talented agricultural writer. It wasn't long before more publications noticed Jefferies. Throughout the 1870s, his work appeared in *Pall Mall Gazette, Globe, Standard, World, Graphic,* and *Cassell's Family Magazine,* with his articles in the last of these catching the attention of the editor of *The Live Stock Journal and Fancier's Gazette,* a weekly publication dedicated to farming.

Breaking out of the limitations of writing for local papers, and having his work in major London publications, must have been exciting for the young Jefferies but, unfortunately, writing in Victorian times, just like today, did not automatically mean fame and fortune. In fact, his first novel, *The Scarlet Shawl*, which was published in 1874, was a critical and financial failure. Nonetheless, with his income from the newspapers and magazines, Jefferies now believed he could live as a professional writer.

In July of the same year, at the age of 25, he was financially secure enough to marry his sweetheart, Jessie Baden. The service took place at Holy Cross Church in nearby Chiseldon. The young couple lived for a short while with Jefferies' parents at Coate, then found a home of their own on Victoria Street, Swindon, where their first child, Richard Harold Jefferies, known as Harold (and nicknamed Toby), was born on 3rd May 1875.

ABOVE: Plaque on the offices of the Wilts and Gloucestershire Standard, in Cirencester. and stone plaque on Jefferies' home in what is now Victoria Road, Swindon.

RIGHT: Holy Cross church, Chiseldon.

Although a new family and home bring joy, they also bring responsibility and for Jefferies this meant the need for a more reliable income. His taste of success with London publishers, and his desire for more, meant that Swindon was no longer the place to live. If he was to get on as a writer, he needed to be nearer the key publishers and editors, as well as the museums, markets, galleries and agricultural shows that only the capital could offer.

After just a year living on Victoria Street, Jefferies went to stay with his Aunt Ellen, in Sydenham, to hunt for a new family home. It was time to leave the countryside, and Wiltshire's agricultural landscape.

LEFT: Agricultural labourer's smock, and yoke.

BELOW: Jefferies' home in Swindon's Old Town - the house is on the left of this row on what is now called Victoria Road.

"Turnips are a favourite food, and leaving the moors the deer wander miles down into the cultivated fields to find them. The stag as he walks across the turnip field bites a turnip, draws it from the ground, and throws it over his shoulders, the jerk detaching the fragment he holds between his teeth, and which is the only portion he touches. He takes but one bite at each turnip, casting the remainder aside in this way, and his course can be traced from one side of the field to the other by the turnips pulled and thrown away after his snatch. In this disdainful manner he damages far more than he actually eats. Hinds eat the turnip down into the ground as a sheep would. A herd of stags or hinds getting into a turnip field will eat broad patches and paths about it. If it is a small field they may destroy every root, and many a farmer visiting his field in the morning has found that every turnip in it has been pulled up and pitched aside by stags in the night. Of potatoes, again, they are very fond, and get at them by scraping away the earth with their fore-feet, or slots, eagerly eating the potatoes thus laid bare. Carrots attract them – almost all animals are fond of carrots, or carrot-tops. Cabbages please them; they will strip a garden of cabbages in no time as clean as possible.

Red Deer

Something Novel

Working for the local newspapers, the prestige of letters in *The Times,* and commissions for London and national publications made for a strong start to a career in writing, even if the pay was not great. However, in his heart, Jefferies had always harboured aspirations to be a novelist, possibly as a result of the sorts of books that he loved to read, with favourites being Homer's *Odyssey,* Cervantes' *Don Quixote*, novels by Walter Scott, and James Fenimore Cooper's *The Pathfinder*, which provided useful fodder for mock battles that the young Jefferies organised among his friends.

Jefferies' first known novel was *Ben Tubbs Adventures,* which he wrote in the attic at Coate Farm while he was still in his teens, though it was not published during his lifetime. His first real attempts at being a novelist came in the mid 1870s as his confidence grew as a professional writer. *The Scarlet Shawl* may have been a disappointment, but it was soon followed up with *Restless Human Hearts* (1875) and *World's End* (1877), all three of them being published by Tinsley Brothers. In the middle of these, Jefferies also wrote *The Rise of Maximin: Emperor of the Orient*, which was published in serial form in *The New Monthly Magazine* during 1876-7. Sadly, none of the novels attained any great sales figures or critical praise.

Nonetheless, Jefferies did not give up on fiction, and even if his earlier novels did not achieve the basic aims of their author, they were a great practice ground for who he was to become. As Edward Thomas puts it: "It must be put to the credit of the form of fiction that Jefferies here and in the other novels has a depth and humanity in his feeling for Nature which are absent from all his early country books. His attempts, however vain, to describe human action and passion led him to search deeps of his own nature that might otherwise have been unsounded; and, almost without value as a whole, his novels were thus an exercise which he could ill have done without, and of considerable use as autobiography."

Perhaps because of the lack of success, or because of his growing reputation as a nature writer, Jefferies took a break from novel writing, not coming back to it until 1880 with the publication of *Greene Ferne Farm*. This met with more favourable reactions, as did *Wood Magic* and *Bevis in 1881-2*, perhaps in some way because of their close affinity with the natural and agricultural worlds which the author was now well known for.

Overall, it was clear to Jefferies, or at least to his publishers, that it was in these arenas where his talents lay – the vivid descriptions of the wildlife he loved so much, and the personal depictions of human life in the countryside he knew so well.

Later on Jefferies was to write three further novels, *The Dewy Morn, After London,* and *Amaryllis at the Fair,* all of them astonishing in their own, original way. In total he wrote eleven novels throughout his life, ten of them being published. But in terms of his career, the fictional world was not going to pay the bills, so Jefferies set off towards London to focus, for now, on work for a number of popular agricultural publications.

LEFT: Jefferies' writing desk, now at the RJ Museum.

RIGHT: A few examples of the many modern editions of Jefferies' novels.

Straw and Stock

In 1877, Jefferies and Jessie, and young Harold, found themselves some 80 miles away from Swindon at 2, Woodside, Tolworth, Surbiton, (now 296 Ewell Road), then on the 'edgelands' of London. Although much developed now, in the 1800s the site of the plain, three-storied terrace house was next to a copse and opposite the local common. So, although he and his family had left rural Coate behind, the writer still had the all important access to countryside that he needed – rich in nature, and in inspiration.

In this new environment, Jefferies settled into regular writing for well known London-based publications, primarily *The Live Stock Journal and Fancier's Gazette,* producing weekly articles on subjects that were of national importance to farmers. Many of the topics are eerily familiar to today, such as issues around American meat, access to water, rising prices, war, hunting, trespass, producers and consumers, weeds and waste, and the importing of cheaper foreign goods.

It is apparent in this work that much of Jefferies' frame of reference was born out of his experiences at Coate and the surrounding area, rather than a detailed knowledge of farming across the country. The articles didn't suffer though, with the writer's increasing skills including an ability to use his local knowledge to paint vivid pictures of broader agricultural issues. And a limited overview did not stop him from making bold and sometimes controversial comments, or from stepping into plainly political arguments. However, he did say, in an article about the dangers of animal disease being carried across borders by armies engaged in the Russo-Turkish War (1877–78), that his "remarks are intended to deal with the agricultural aspect of the war only, and not as expressing an opinion upon political complications."

ABOVE: 'After London II (Richard Jefferies on Tolworth Court Farm),' by Lucy Furlong.

RIGHT: The reaping hook or sickle, used for 'vagging' straw, was such an important tool that Jefferies referred to as "the very symbol of agriculture."

BACKGROUND: The mixed-use "straw and stock" landscape of Aldbourne, Wiltshire.

With farmers and landowners being the core target audience, much of Jefferies' professional writing was embedded in the same Conservative politics as *The Times* letters. But if the articles reflected Jefferies' views at the time, his later writings were to show a whole other side to his thinking. Perhaps such closeness to the subjects gave him a new depth of understanding about the land and, crucially, the people who lived and worked on it.

One of the subjects which occurred regularly in Jefferies' articles related to the different needs of arable and animal farming, seen by some as a split between the 'wet' west and the 'dry' east. But Jefferies was used to these sorts of contradictions: he had been born in rural, agricultural Wiltshire, but had also spent plenty of time in 'society' with his aunt Ellen in London's suburbs – he believed answers lay somewhere between any two poles, both in agriculture and in people.

"In the way of sheer, downright force few effects of machinery are more striking than a steam-ploughing engine dragging the shares across a wide expanse of stiff clay. The huge engines used in our ironclad vessels work with a graceful ease which deceives the eye; the ponderous cranks revolve so smoothly, and shine so brightly with oil and polish, that the mind is apt to underrate the work performed. But these ploughing engines stand out solitary and apart from other machinery, and their shape itself suggests crude force, such force as may have existed in the mastodon or other unwieldy monster of the prehistoric ages. The broad wheels sink into the earth under the pressure; the steam hissing from the escape valves is carried by the breeze through the hawthorn hedge, hiding the red berries with a strange, unwonted cloud; the thick dark brown smoke, rising from the funnel as the stoker casts its food of coal into the fiery mouth of the beast, falls again and floats heavily over the yellow stubble, smothering and driving away the partridges and hares.

There is a smell of oil, and cotton-waste, and gas, and steam, and smoke, which overcomes the fresh, sweet odour of the earth and green things after a shower. Stray lumps of coal crush the delicate pimpernel and creeping convolvulus. A shrill, short scream rushes forth and echoes back from an adjacent rick-puff! The fly-wheel revolves, and the drum underneath tightens its hold upon the wire rope. Across yonder a curious, shapeless thing, with a man riding upon it, comes jerking forward, tearing its way through stubble and clay, dragging its iron teeth with sheer strength deep through the solid earth. The thick wire rope stretches and strains as if it would snap and curl up like a tortured snake; the engine pants loudly and quick; the plough now glides forward, now pauses, and, as it were, eats its way through a tougher place, then glides again, and presently there is a pause, and behold the long furrow with the upturned subsoil is completed. A brief pause, and back it travels again, this time drawn from the other side, where a twin monster puffs and pants and belches smoke, while the one that has done its work uncoils its metal sinews. When the furrows run up and down a slope, the savage force, the fierce, remorseless energy of the engine pulling the plough upwards, gives an idea of power which cannot but impress the mind."

Unequal Agriculture

RIGHT: *Small cider barrel for taking to work.*

OPPOSITE: *Vintage steam traction engine owned by Colin Hatch, at the Richard Jefferies Museum.*

62

Victorian Agriculture

Between 1750 and 1850 huge changes occurred in British agriculture – a seismic shift away from family-run smallholdings to more intensive semi-mechanised production. This led to greater food output, which in turn led to a growth in population. With millions more mouths to feed, the traditional subsistence economy, where individual growers sold the little surplus they had for tools and other goods, became outdated and inadequate. With the advent of the Enclosure Acts, which began in the 1750s, smaller strips of farmland were amalgamated by landlords to create larger fields, bordered by hedges. This consolidation of land meant rent was raised per acre and attracted a new kind of tenant farmer who could afford to pay more and was more capitalist in outlook. The desire and need for profit drove experimentation with technological innovation, such as crop rotation, and the use of crops like turnip and clover to release nitrogen into the soil.

Farmland production intensified and more land was brought into agricultural usage; woodland was felled, fenland was drained in the East of England, and areas of common pasture land decreased as arable became more profitable. Grain was, as ever, in high demand for bread and beer, the two dietary staples, especially for the lower classes. By 1870, over 30% of Wiltshire's agricultural land was given over to corn and this made Wiltshire's agricultural economy vulnerable as the price of corn fluctuated. Towards the end of the nineteenth century, bacon and cheese also became key produce due to uncertainty about the profitably of corn and sheep, the two commodities which had dominated Wiltshire's rural economy for decades. However, while the amount of food being produced was rising, the number of people working in agriculture was decreasing, because higher yields meant each worker was producing more food. In Swindon, this meant many workers moved into the town to find work on the railways where pay could be better, even if the cost of living was higher in such urban areas.

The nineteenth century agrarian economy was a well organised hierarchy with landowners at the top, capitalist tenant farmers in the middle and labourers at the bottom. Agriculture had transformed to become a profitable enterprise; produce was a commodity to sell rather than a means of subsistence. At the bottom of this rural hierarchy, farm labourers were paid daily, even if working at the same place for a season. Wages on farms were higher in summer than winter, reflecting the fact that there was more work in the summer harvest months. But these inconsistencies were not easy for the tenant farmers either, and with variations in crop prices and taxes, and changes from leases-for-life to annual rent, farming was not an easy industry in Victorian times.

"Cotton, coal, and iron cannot be eaten, but the land gives us corn and beef; therefore, the land stands first and foremost, and the agriculturist, as the tiller of land, possesses an inalienable right which it is his duty to maintain, and in so doing he is acting for the good of the community. I believe that the son and the daughter should obey their parents, and show regard to their wishes even when legally independent. Also that the servant should obey his employer.

The connection between employer and employed does not cease with the payment of wages. It is the duty of the servant to show consideration for the advice of the master; and the master is not free from responsibility as to the education and the comfort of the man. The master is bound by all laws, human and Divine, to pay a fair amount of wages for a day's work. If he does not do so he robs the workman as much as if he stole the money from his pocket. The workman is equally bound to do his work properly, and in neglecting to do so he robs his employer. To demand more wages than has been earned is an attempt at robbery. Both master and man should respect authority, and abide by its decisions."

The Farmer at Home

"It is a fact that English dairymaids, many years ago, made very good butter, though possessing only what would now be thought the most primitive appliances, and guided by a traditionary rule of thumb. There are places even at this day where an excellent article is produced in the same old style, and where nothing marked 'patent' has ever penetrated. But while they certainly did make good butter, there is another fact equally certain, i.e., that there were hardly two dairies to be found which sent forth butter of the same quality. That from one farm was really delicious, and that from another almost adjoining was simply detestable. It may be said that the same is the case now; so it is, with an important difference - taking ten dairies, the proportion producing poor butter is perhaps double what it used to be. By dairies are here meant ordinary farm dairies, the butter from which of recent years has greatly deteriorated - a few special districts, of course, excepted.

In short, butter-making in the old style is a lost art, which it is useless to attempt to revive, for the reason that to achieve commercial success in these times there must be uniformity of production. Instead of a few dairies making, for a time, an excellent article, they must *all* endeavour to manufacture a saleable commodity, or they must perforce let the task alone. Success under the old system depended entirely upon personal character, personal knowledge, and even personal peculiarities, such as the accident of having cold hands. As in the nature of things there could never be more than a certain proportion of persons so gifted, it followed that the produce of the dairies must be of a most irregular description.

At the present day the manufacturer cannot afford to depend wholly and solely upon the vague chance of securing a clever manipulator; he must have uniformity, and must be able to rely upon it, and that uniformity can only be attained by mechanical means. There is, therefore, everywhere an increasing tendency to substitute machinery for manual dexterity, and a scientific process for one based purely on custom. But such facts as have been established by the experience of years have not been ignored; it is, indeed, rather by investigation into the causes which brings about well-known effects, than by altogether independent discovery, that progress has been made. What the clever dairymaid of a generation ago did morning after morning simply because she had 'heard tell' it was the best method, we want now to analyse, to find the reason why and wherefore, with the object of producing the same result with absolute certainty."

The Future of the Dairy

ABOVE: Butter paddles.

RIGHT: Butter churn and roller, and abandoned cowsheds at Coate Farm in the 1950s.

Hunting Country

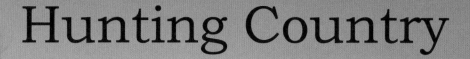

As well as growing crops and raising livestock, Victorian rural life was also dominated by hunting, both for necessary pest control, and for food. Jefferies grew up with this; to him, the trapping or shooting of vermin, such as rats, weasels, foxes, and birds of prey, and the hunting of edible animals such as pheasants and rabbits, were simply accepted daily activities in the country. But it wasn't only the practical reasons: hunting, particularly shooting and fishing, was also good sport, which Jefferies enjoyed from his earliest youth. In *Bevis*, the character Mark says: "This is the jolliest day we've had. All shooting and killing and real hunting – and no work and no cooking, except just what we like. It's splendid."

To Victorian landowners the sport of hunting was as important as the agriculture itself, not only providing a further income but also bringing wealthy and influential people to country estates. As Jefferies describes in his 1879 book *The Amateur Poacher,* "Everything was prepared to attract the wealthy man who wanted the temporary use of a good country house, first-class shooting and hunting." For Jefferies' writing this was a rich area full of fascinating, and gory, details to titillate his readership. Importantly, the material gave the writer scope for more creativity, describing not only the facts, but the characters and feelings associated with such visceral subjects. Around the same time, the *Pall Mall Gazette* published another series of articles, which became *The Gamekeeper at Home.* This covers a period of time when Jefferies 'shadowed' Benny Haylock, the gamekeeper of the Burderop estate, near Coate. A reviewer at the time described it as "displaying much knowledge, much love of the subject, and no small amount of literary power," while Edward Thomas called it "the first thoroughly rustic book in English, by a countryman and about the country."

"The man's instinct for hunting was so strong that it seemed to overcome everything else."

The Amateur Poacher

ABOVE: At over a metre in length this lethal 'gin' trap is big enough to catch large prey, and might also trap unwary human visitors.

BACKGROUND: Mist rolling down across Broome Manor from the Burderop estate.

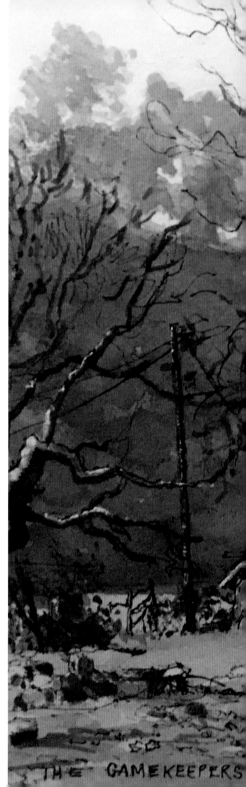

The keeper's cottage stands in a sheltered "coombe," or narrow hollow of the woodlands, overshadowed by a mighty Spanish chestnut, bare now of leaves, but in summer a noble tree. The ash wood covers the slope at the rear; on one side is a garden, and on the other a long strip of meadow with elms. In front, and somewhat lower, a streamlet winds, fringing the sward, and across it the fir plantations begin, their dark sombre foliage hanging over the water.

A dead willow trunk thrown from bank to bank forms a rude bridge; the tree, not even squared, gives little surface for the foot, and in frosty weather a slip is easy. From this primitive contrivance a path, out of which others fork, leads into the intricacies of the covers, and from the garden a wicket gate opens on the ash wood. The elms in the meadow are full of rooks' nests, and in the spring the coombe will resound with their cawing; these black bandits, who do not touch it at other times, will then ravage the garden to feed their hungry young, despite ingenious scarecrows. A row of kennels, tenanted by a dozen dogs, extends behind the cottage: lean retrievers yet unbroken, yelping spaniels, pointers, and perhaps a few greyhounds or fancy breeds, if "young master" has a taste that way.

Beside the kennels is a shed ornamented with rows upon rows of dead and dried vermin, furred and feathered, impaled for their misdeeds; and over the door a couple of horseshoes nailed for luck – a superstition yet lingering in the by-ways of the woods and hills. Within are the ferret hutches, warm and dry; for the ferret is a shivery creature, and likes nothing so well as to nozzle down in a coat-pocket with a little hay. Here are spades and billhooks, twine and rabbit nets, traps, and other odds and ends scattered about with the wires and poacher's implements impounded from time to time."

The Gamekeeper at Home

RIGHT: The gamekeeper's cottage painted by Frank Quinton in 1995.

OTTAGE, HODSON

73

"Dickon is long and rawboned, a powerful fellow, strong of limb, and twice my build; but he sips too often at the brown brandy, and after the first burst I can head him. But he knows the hills and the route the hare will take, so that I have but to keep pace. In five minutes as we cross a ridge we see the game again; the hare is circling back – she passes under us not fifty yards away, as we stand panting on the hill.

The youngest hound gains, and runs right over her; she doubles, the older hound picks up the running. By a furze-bush she doubles again; but the young one turns her – the next moment she is in the jaws of the old dog.

Again and again the hounds are slipped, now one couple, now the other: we pant, and can scarcely speak with running, but the wild excitement of the hour and the sweet pure air of the Downs supply fresh strength. The little lad brings the mare anywhere: through the furze, among the flint-pits, jolting over the ruts, she rattles along with sure alacrity. There are five hares in the sack under the straw when at last we get up and slowly drive down to the highway, reaching it some two miles from where we left it."

The Amateur Poacher

"Here the green drive shows traces of the poaching it received from the thick-planted hoofs of the hunt when the leaves were off and the blast of the horn sounded fitfully as the gale carried the sound away. The vixen is now at peace, though perhaps it would scarcely be safe to wander too near the close-shaven mead where the keeper is occupied more and more every day with his pheasant-hatching. And far down on the lonely outlying farms, where even in fox-hunting England the music of the hounds is hardly heard in three years (because no great coverts cause the run to take that way), foul murder is sometimes done on Reynard or his family. A hedge-cutter marks the sleeping-place in the withies where the fox curls up by day; and with his rusty gun, that sometimes slaughters a roaming pheasant, sends the shot through the red side of the slumbering animal. Then, thrust ignobly into a sack, he shoulders the fox and marches round from door to door, tumbling the limp body rudely down on the pitching stones to prove that the fowls will now be safe, and to be rewarded with beer and small coin. A dead fox is profit to him for a fortnight. These evil deeds of course are cloaked as far as possible."

The Amateur Poacher

Victorian London

Until the 1600s Greater London was no larger than one square mile; today, it covers an area of around 600 square miles. One of the most significant periods of expansion in its history was in the nineteenth century – by 1815 London was already the biggest city in the world, and by 1860 its population had swelled to over 3 million. At least one in three of the residents had not been born in the city and many of these were economic migrants – including Jefferies, in his own small way. The changes in agriculture he had seen first-hand had driven thousands of landless labourers into the cities to seek work.

London was a city of contrasts. On the one hand it was a dazzling display of all that was new and modern. By 1870, Pugin's iconic Gothic revival Houses of Parliament sat centre stage on the banks of the Thames. The London Underground (pictured opposite) was the first of its kind when it opened in 1863. The City of London was the economic capital of the world, and the Great Exhibition of 1851 showcased Britain's industrial strength and imperial prowess. The upper classes and burgeoning middle classes could spend their disposable income at stores such as Harrods which was founded in 1849. In her domestic bible, the *Book of Household Management*, Mrs Beeton instructed aspirational women how to host afternoon tea. But London's veneer of respectability was thin. The calm cleanliness and order which she describes in the middle-class household would have been alien to anyone living in the slums.

The reality was that for the majority of the inhabitants of London, life was precarious and dangerous. The horror of poverty portrayed in Dicken's novels was fact not fiction. Overcrowding and unsanitary conditions facilitated the spread of diseases such as cholera typhus and tuberculosis. Crime was rife, prisons were overcrowded and their regimes harsh. The Great Stink of 1858, where Parliament was forced to curtail some of its business because of the stench emanating from the polluted river Thames, brought London's shameful public health problems to the noses of upper and middle-class politicians. But the real saviours of the poor, who endured pestilence and social misery, were men such as Jon Snow, who recognised the link between dirty water and cholera, and Joseph Bazalgette who pioneered London's first system of sewers.

Despite these efforts, change was piecemeal and inadequate. In the 1890s shipping magnate and philanthropist Charles Booth and his team collated first hand evidence which mapped the socio-economic conditions of London's inhabitants. The study was called an *Enquiry into Life and Labour in London* (1886-1903), and colour-coded London according to the social situation of its inhabitants. Maps made from the research coloured the poorest houses in black, many of them, and the people living in them described as: 'Lowest class. Vicious, semi-criminal'. The findings shocked everyone, and considerable momentum to the calls for social welfare reform.

BACKGROUND: Photograph of Jefferies aged 30, captured in June 1879 by London Stereoscopic Company.

Nature

Nature of the Country

Jefferies' few years in Surbiton were the best of his life. With his meagre but regular income he and Jessie were able to enjoy family life, with young Harold growing fast and a second child arriving on 6th December 1880 – a daughter named Jessie after her mother but known by her second name, Phyllis. And for Jefferies himself, the time saw him grow from little-known Wiltshire journalist to writer of national repute. Over four years, from 1877 to 1882, Jefferies had countless articles and essays published as well as the country life books, *The Gamekeeper at Home, Wild Life in a Southern County, The Amateur Poacher, Round About a Great Estate,* and *Hodge and His Masters*. On top of this, Jefferies wrote his two children's books, *Wood Magic* and *Bevis*, and a well-received minor novel, *Greene Ferne Farm*. These works led to Jefferies being compared with the great English nature writer, Gilbert White. One of the time's top literary critics, Q.D. Leavis, called *Round About a Great Estate* "one of the most delightful books in the English language."

There is, unsurprisingly, one element that runs through all of Jefferies' books, even where the title or genre suggest something different: nature itself. Jefferies was not a scientist, but his time in the countryside, in Wiltshire and in Surbiton, taught him a tremendous amount about natural life. He wrote about every living thing: birds, mammals, insects, trees, flowers, and fish. And he wrote about every other aspect of nature too, including earth, water, sun, moon and space. Jefferies was, essentially, an ecologist. He may not have studied formally, but all his observations related to the interactions between living things and their physical environment – the very definition of ecology. For Jefferies, the relationship between humans and other living things was paramount. He was as interested in human ecology – our environment and interactions – as he was in nature. But a fascination with both humans and the natural world led to conflicts and contradictions. For example, we know that Jefferies loved hunting, which was part of his world, but his feelings were not always clear cut. It wasn't only poachers committing "foul murder" on foxes that troubled the writer. As he tells us in *The Open Air*: "The shameless way in which every otter that dares to show itself is shot, trapped, beaten to death, and literally battered out of existence, should rouse the indignation of every sportsman and every lover of nature."

Writing in genteel Surrey may have been an influence, but the dominance of this nature-loving side of Jefferies is encapsulated in a moment back in Wiltshire during which the beauty of a pheasant overrides his intention to kill it. The quote, from *The Amateur Poacher,* is given on the next page.

ABOVE: Plaque on the building where Jefferies' Tolworth house once stood.

OPPOSITE: Early editions of some of Jefferies' Surbiton works, pictured in the parlour of the house at Coate..

"A reason why people frequently miss pheasants in cover-shooting, despite of their size, is because they look at the body, the wings, and the tail. But if they looked only at the head, and thought of that, very few would escape. My finger felt the trigger, and the least increase of pressure would have been fatal; but in the act I hesitated, dropped the barrel, and watched the beautiful bird.

That watching so often stayed the shot that at last it grew to be a habit: the mere simple pleasure of seeing birds and animals, when they were quite unconscious that they were observed, being too great to be spoilt by the discharge. After carefully getting a wire over a jack; after waiting in a tree till a hare came along; after sitting in a mound till the partridges began to run together to roost; in the end the wire or gun remained unused. The same feeling has equally checked my hand in legitimate shooting: time after time I have flushed partridges without firing, and have let the hare bound over the furrow free.

I have entered many woods just for the pleasure of creeping through the brake and the thickets. Destruction in itself was not the motive; it was an overpowering instinct for woods and fields."

The Amateur Poacher

Habits of Bird or Animal

In May 1878 Jefferies makes an entry in his notebook about a series of articles for The Pall Mall Gazette to be called *Wild Life of a Southern County*. On the next page he changes *of* to *in* and, perhaps more importantly, he also defends the title, explaining: "In evidence why? thought – I have explained at once what the wild life is so that the title shall convey no false impression." The defence was possibly in answer to criticism or questioning from the editor of the newspaper, given that the note was made just a week or two before the first instalment, or maybe Jefferies was just jotting down his musings about the title for himself. Either way, he clearly felt the phrase *wild life* might be misconstrued. This is because he was employing it in an unusual way, the phrase being more generally used at that time to describe either excesses of human behaviour, or new worlds being discovered beyond what was called civilisation.

In fact Jefferies was really using the term in both of these senses, but with his own twist. Firstly, there was something for him about the freedom, the 'wildness' of nature. This was close to the accepted use of the words as something bacchanalian, except the author applied them to birds and animals not drunken humans: "The joy in life of these animals – indeed, of almost all animals and birds in freedom – is very great. You may see it in every motion: in the lissom bound of the hare, the playful leap of the rabbit, the song that the lark and the finch must sing; the soft, loving coo of the dove in the hawthorn; the blackbird ruffling out his feathers on a rail. The sense of living – the consciousness of seeing and feeling – is manifestly intense in them all, and is in itself an exquisite pleasure. Their appetites seem ever fresh: they rush to the banquet spread by Mother Earth with a gusto that Lucullus never knew in the midst of his artistic gluttony; they drink from the stream with dainty sips as though it were richest wine." Secondly, Jefferies steals the phrase away from the grand discoveries of unknown continents, and gives it instead to the world that is right here on our doorstep, in the fields and streams around us, under the eaves and skirting boards of our homes: "There is a frontier line to civilisation in this country yet, and not far outside its great centres we come quickly even now on the borderland of nature. Modern progress, except where it has exterminated them, has scarcely touched the habits of bird or animal; so almost up to the very houses of the metropolis the nightingale yearly returns to her former haunts."

The idea of Mother Earth providing a banquet is a key element of Jefferies' use of *wild life*, alluding to the inextricable relationships between different creatures, and to their habitats – the study of which today would come under the term ecology. And he goes further, reminding us that *our* world is part of that ecology.

In the preface to the 1879 book version of *Wild Life in a Southern County*, Jefferies explains that the work is arranged by "the contour of the country", since even a bird as common as a starling cannot be described without reference to its habitat: "it cannot be separated from the farmhouse in the thatch of which it often breeds, the rooks with whom it associates, or the friendly sheep upon whose backs it sometimes rides."

Perhaps because of Jefferies' particular slant on the words, or maybe because the book made the phrase familiar to so many people (it continued to be published regularly for more than sixty years) the book title is given as the earliest example in the Oxford English Dictionary of *wild life* being used in a nature context. It seems fitting to think of Jefferies, for whom the natural world was so important, playing such a notable, pioneering role in the evolution of the phrase which we know today as a single word, *wildlife*.

NOTE: In 1888, in his *Eulogy of Richard Jefferies*, the writer Walter Besant says: "His work, as well as his days, must be concerning the fields and the wild life." In 1909, Edward Thomas adds a hyphen to the term in his book, *Richard Jefferies: His Life and Work,* reiterating Jefferies' simple message: "all wild-life should be encouraged and protected." In more modern times, authors Richard Mabey and Ben Macdonald both name *Wild Life in a Southern County* as their earliest introduction to the art of nature writing.

LEFT: Watercolour by H. C. Babington depicting the rich wild life characters of 'Wood Magic.'

Stream of Birds

In Jefferies' observations of wild creatures, birds seem to dominate. This is perhaps understandable given their higher visibility compared to most wildlife. Jefferies mentions over a hundred species which he knew well from his regular walks, with just as many birds to see in urban Tolworth as in rural Swindon.

The edge of London may not have generated the same temptation to go great distances as in the countryside, but Jefferies would still cover miles every day, exploring bird-life and other nature around the area. His regular timetable started with an hour and a half walk each morning, returning home for lunch and some work, and then another walk in the afternoon. He also liked to break his habit sometimes and go out at odd times, often to the same places that he had visited many times before. As back on Liddington Hill, such nature walks let him escape what he called "the constant routine of house-life, the same work, the same thought in the work, the little circumstances regularly recurring... which will dull the keenest edge of thought."

To someone so ecologically-minded as Jefferies, it was fascinating to discover that a city was as good a habitat for birds as any country field or woodland. Edward Thomas sums up the writer's amazement at the birds of Surbiton, and of London suburbs in general: "In his first spring there he was 'astonished and delighted,' by the richness of the bird-life; he never knew so many nightingales. He saw herons go over, and a teal. Magpies were common, and he records ten together on September 9, 1881, within twelve miles of Charing Cross. There were the same happy greenfinches – his favourite birds – which 'never cease love-making in the elms.' The beautiful white bryony grew over the hedges. 'Birds,' he notes, 'care nothing for appropriate surroundings.' Almost at his door was a copse of Scotch and spruce fir, hornbeam, birch, and ash – now vanished – where he used to watch dove and pigeon, cuckoo, nightingale, sedge-warbler, and missel-thrush. Once a pair of house-martins built under his eaves, and the starlings were welcome, though they dammed the gutter."

RIGHT: Taxidermy missel-thrush. In 'Nature Near London,'
Jefferies describes the missel-thrush as "the trumpeter of spring:
Lord of March, his proud call challenges the woods; there are
none who can answer."

"My preconceived views on the subject were quite overthrown by the presence of as much bird-life as I had been accustomed to in distant fields and woods."

Nature Near London

89

"Only a very few days since – it does not seem a week – there was a chiffchaff calling in a copse as merrily as in the spring. This little bird is the first, or very nearly the first, to come in the spring, and one of the last to go as autumn approaches. It is curious that, though singled out as a first sign of spring, the chiffchaff has never entered into the home life of the people like the robin, the swallow, or even the sparrow.

There is nothing about it in the nursery rhymes or stories, no one goes out to listen to it, children are not taught to recognise it, and grown-up persons are often quite unaware of it."

Nature Near London

"This hollow at Long Ditton is the very place of singing birds; never was such a place for singing – the valley is full of music. In the oaks blackbirds whistle. You do not often see them; they are concealed by the thick foliage up on high, for they seek the top branches, which are more leafy; but once now and then they quietly flutter across to another perch. The blackbird's whistle is very human, like a human being playing the flute; an uncertain player, now drawing forth a bar of a beautiful melody and then losing it again. He does not know what quiver or what turn his note will take before it ends; the note leads him and completes itself."

Nature Near London

"This hawk has a light easy flight, usually maintaining an altitude a little lower than the tallest elms, but higher than most trees. He will keep this particular altitude for hours together, and sweep over miles of country, with only occasional variations – excluding, of course, descents for the purpose of taking mice. It is usually at this height that a kestrel hovers, though he is capable of doing it at much greater elevation. As he comes gliding through the atmosphere, suddenly he shoots up a little (say, roughly, two or three feet), and then stops short. His tail, which is broader than it looks, is bent slightly downwards; his wings beat the air, at the first glance, just as if he was progressing. Sometimes he seems to oscillate to one side, sometimes to the other; but these side movements do not amount to any appreciable change of position. If there be little or no wind (note this) he remains beating the air, to the eye at least perfectly stationary, perhaps as much as half a minute or more. He then seems to slip forward about half a yard, as if a pent-up force was released, but immediately recovers himself and hovers again."

The Hovering of the Kestrel

"But although the night seems the heron's principal feeding time, he frequently fishes in the day. Generally, his long neck enables him to see danger, but not always. Several times I have come right on a heron, when the banks of the brook were high and the bushes thick, before he has seen me, so as to be for the moment within five yards. His clumsy terror is quite ludicrous: try how he will he cannot fly fast at starting; he requires fifty yards to get properly underway."

Wild Life in a Southern County

As a shower falls from the sky, so falls the song of the larks. There is no end to them: they are everywhere; over every acre away across the plain to the downs, and up on the highest hill. Every crust of English bread has been sung over at its birth in the green blade by a lark."

Field and Hedgerow

"The spot the wild geese used to visit in the winter is still remembered, though they come there no more; drains and cultivation having driven them away from that southern district. In the course of the winter, perhaps, a small flock may be seen at a great height passing over, but they do not alight, and in some years are not observed at all."

The Gamekeeper at Home

"If but by reason and will I could reach the godlike calm and courage of what we so thoughtlessly call the timid turtle-dove, I should lead a nearly perfect life."

The Life of the Fields

97

Boldest Beasts

Having been brought up on a farm and lived so much of his life in an agricultural community, it is no surprise that the majority of the animals (mammals, fish and amphibians) Jefferies wrote about were those which were common to that world. But although agricultural land, with its neat fields, hedge boundaries and maintained woodlands, looks like a natural environment, it is, in reality, an industrial landscape. Consequently, only certain wild species are found there and it was these that Jefferies

observed most of all. In describing a deer-park, he says "The list of animals still living within the pale and still wild is short indeed. Besides the deer, which are not wild, there are hares, rabbits, squirrels, two kinds of rat, – the land and the water rat, – stoat, weasel, mole, and mouse. There are more varieties of mouse than of any other animal: these, the weakest of all, have escaped best, though exposed to so many enemies. A few foxes, and still fewer badgers, complete the list, for there are no other animals here. Modern times are fatal to all creatures of prey, whether furred or feathered; and so even the owls are less numerous, both in actual numbers and in variety of species, than they were even fifty years ago."

Several times in his works he mentions a lack of creatures, such as the demise of the polecat – or fitchew, as it was known, – the vanishing of the marten, and the increasing rarity of the badger: "It is curious that the badger has lived on through sufferance for three centuries. Nearly three centuries ago, a chronicler observed that the badger would have been rooted out before his time had it not been for the parks. There was no great store of badgers then; there is no great store now."

Through trips to new and further afield places, Jefferies did observe animals in wilder habitats, including, for example, otters and red deer. And of course his years living among farm animals provided rich pickings, with cows, horses, goats, chickens and a donkey. The children's novel *Wood Magic* is very obviously based on Coate Farm, and includes detailed impressions of all manner of wildlife. The lead roles go to birds, but they are supported by a cast which embraces the fox, weasel, mouse, toad, squirrel and rabbit, plus fish in the brook, a "very cunning spider", and Hur-hur the pig, who presumably lived in the sty that still exists on the site today. The animals are anthropomorphised, although carefully within the limits of their natural tendencies, and give us as much a view into Jefferies view of human 'politics' as they do about his thoughts on the creatures themselves.

ABOVE LEFT: Painting of bulls by Richard's sister, Sarah.

LEFT: Pigsty at Coate Farm.

99

"Iden set traps for mice in the cellar and the larder, and slew them there without mercy. He picked up the trap, swung it round, opening the door at the same instant, and the wretched captive was dashed to death upon the stone flags of the floor. So he hated them and persecuted them in one place, and fed them in another. A long psychological discussion might be held on this apparent inconsistency, but I shall leave analysis to those who like it, and go on recording facts. I will only make one remark. That nothing is consistent that is human. If it was not inconsistent it would have no association with a living person. From the merest thin slit, as it were, between his eyelids, Iden watched the mice feed and run about his knees till, having eaten every crumb, they descended his leg to the floor."

Amaryllis at the Fair

"With such animosity has the otter been hunted that he is becoming one of the rarest of wild animals here in the south. He is practically extinct on the majority of southern streams, and has been almost beaten off the Thames itself. But the otter is not likely to be exterminated in the sense that the wolf has been. Otters will be found elsewhere in England long after the last of them has disappeared from the south."

The Life of the Fields

"By the shore, on this, the sunny side of the bridge, a few forget-me-nots grow in their season, water crow's-foot flowers, flags lie along the surface and slowly swing from side to side like a boat at anchor. The breeze brings a ripple, and the sunlight sparkles on it, the light reflected dances up the piers of the bridge. Those that pass along the road are naturally drawn to this bright parapet where the brook runs brimming full through green meadows. You can see right to the bottom; you can see where the rush of the water has scooped out a deeper channel under the arches, but look as long as you like, there are no fish.

The trout I watched so long and with such pleasure, was always on the other side, at the tail of the arch, waiting for whatever might come through to him. There in perpetual shadow he lay in wait, a little at the side of the arch, scarcely ever varying his position except to dart a yard up under the bridge to seize anything, and drifting out again to bring up at his anchorage, if people looked over the parapet that side they did not see him; they could not see the bottom there for the shadow, or if the summer noonday cast a strong beam, even then it seemed to cover the surface of the water with a film of light which could not be seen through. There are some aspects from which even a picture hung on a wall close at hand cannot be seen. So no one saw the trout; if anyone more curious leant over the parapet he was gone in a moment under the arch. "

A London Trout

"The brooks have ceased to run. There is no music now at the old hatch where we used to sit in danger of our lives, happy as kings, on the narrow bar over the deep water. The barred pike that used to come up in such numbers are no more among the flags. The perch used to drift down the stream, and then bring up again. The sun shone there for a very long time, and the water rippled and sang, and it always seemed to me that I could feel the rippling and the singing and the sparkling back through the centuries. The brook is dead, for when man goes nature ends. I dare say there is water there still, but it is not the brook; the brook is gone like John Brown's soul."

My Old Village

"There is no more beautiful creature than a stag in his pride of antler, his coat of ruddy gold, his grace of form and motion. He seems the natural owner of the ferny coombes, the oak woods, the broad slopes of heather. They belong to him, and he steps upon the sward in lordly mastership. The land is his, and the hills, the sweet streams, and rocky glens. He is infinitely more natural than the cattle and sheep that have strayed into his domains. For some inexplicable reason, although they too are in reality natural, when he is present they look as if they had been put there and were kept there by artificial means. They do not, as painters say, shade in with the colours and shape of the landscape. He is as natural as an oak, or a fern, or a rock itself. He is earth-born – autochthon – and holds possession by descent. Utterly scorning control, the walls and hedges are nothing to him – he roams where he chooses, as fancy leads, and gathers the food that pleases him. . . ."

Red Deer

"The best time to enter such a hiding-place is a little before the sun sinks: for as his beams turn red all the creatures that rest during the day begin to stir. Then the hares start down from the uplands and appear on the short stubble, where the level rays throw exaggerated shadows behind them. When six or eight hares are thus seen near the centre of a single field, they and their shadows seem to take possession of and occupy it."

Field and Hedgerow

"In the furze on Tolworth Common – a resort of chats – the land-lizards are busy every sunny day. They run over the bunches of dead, dry grass – quite white and blanched – grasping it in their claws, like a monkey with hands and prehensile feet. They are much swifter than would be supposed. There was one on the sward by the Ewell road the other morning, quite without a tail; the creature was as quick as possible, but the grass too short to hide under till it reached some nettles."

The Hills and Vale

But it is the same in reality with the creatures on the earth. There are some of these even now to which use has not accustomed the mind. Such, for instance, as the toad. At its shapeless shape appearing in an unexpected corner many people start and exclaim. They are aware that they shall receive no injury from it, yet it affrights them, it sends a shock to the mind. The reason lies in its obviously anti-human character. All the designless, formless chaos of chance-directed matter, without idea or human plan, squats there embodied in the pathway. By watching the creature, and convincing the mind from observation that it is harmless, and even has uses, the horror wears away. But still remains the form to which the mind can never reconcile itself."

The Story of My Heart

No Settled Home

Not long after moving to Surbiton, Jefferies would have had the news that the family he had left behind had to move out of Coate Farm. Unfortunately, Jefferies' father – James Luckett Jefferies – was struggling with the £1,500 mortgage he'd had to take out to keep the property after his own father died in 1868. Over time the debt had grown, eventually totalling £2,750 despite interest payments being kept up. After more than a year on the market, the farm was sold in September 1878 to the Dean and Chapter of Westminster, which then sold the house on to neighbouring landowners, the Goslings.

Jefferies' writing suggests that he had very mixed feelings about 'home', and the portraits he gives of his parents as Mr and Mrs Iden in *Amaryllis at the Fair*, suggest he had a mixed relationship with them too. His London-born mother, Elizabeth (Betsy) Gyde, had never really taken to the world of her farmer husband, she was: "a town-bred woman with a beautiful face and a pleasure-loving soul, kind and generous to a fault, but unsuited to a country life." Meanwhile, his father, James, was a curious mixture of someone who was fascinated by the world and loved his garden, but not able to make a financial success of the farm. After the sale of the property he became a jobbing gardener, with the couple ending up living in Bath. However, although Jefferies could not visit Coate anymore, his father did visit him. In

July 1879, while resident at a lodging house on King Street, Bath, Jefferies senior describes a three-week stay in Surbiton, and makes a few comments about his son's writing: "When I first came to Bath soon after being with him I was highly amused to hear discussions who ever could be the writer when he first began writing articles in the Standard I occasionally saw and read one, and I was quite in a rage I knew it was words that I had spoken but I had no idea R J was the person and he never mentioned it." Perhaps

Jefferies failed to mention his work because he knew it would not always command parental praise and pride.

To Jefferies, the childhood home was filled with mixed memories: on the one hand, adventures around Coate Water and exploration of the nearby countryside; on the other, financial hardship and family unhappiness. To use a line from *After London*: "The whole place was thus falling to decay, while at the same time it seemed to be flowing with milk and honey."

Strangely, the author barely mentions his three siblings in his work, but of course there were the non-human companions like Pan, a spaniel who appears in the childhood world of Bevis, and, later, a pointer who accompanied Jefferies on his walks.

LEFT: The main house at Coate Farm, painted by Kate Tryon in 1910 after the Jefferies family had moved out.

RIGHT: Particulars of the estate in 1877 when it was put up for sale.

PARTICULARS.

ALL THAT

FREEHOLD & COMPACT ESTATE,

Situate at Coate, in the Parish of Chisledon, Wilts,

Within two miles of the Market Town of Swindon, now and for many years in the occupation of Mr. JAMES JEFFERIES,

COMPRISING A COMFORTABLE

DWELLING-HOUSE,

Containing Sitting Room, Parlour, 4 Bed Rooms, and 2 Attics, Dairy, Good Cellar, and the usual Domestic Offices, together with

ORCHARD, GARDEN,

STABLES, CONVENIENT CATTLE SHEDS, AND YARDS,

AND SEVERAL CLOSES OF

RICH PASTURE LAND,

Containing 36a. 1r. 25p., or thereabouts, as follows :

No. on Tithe Map.	NAME.	STATE.	A.	R.	P.
210º	Upper Stamps Ground	Pasture ...	1	3	18
208*	Lower Stamps Ground	Ditto ...	1	3	18
220	Road Ground, Cow Pen, and Rick Yard	Ditto ...	5	1	14
225	Little Axe, (commonly called Little Hawkes)	Pasture ...	1	3	34
225A	Double Mound round ditto, and Withy Bed ...	... ...	0	3	20
226	Great Axe, (commonly called Great Hawkes) ...	Pasture ...	9	0	30
211º	Sterts Marsh	Ditto ...	4	3	22
125	Homestead, Cow Shed, and Yards adjoining ...	... ...	0	1	39
123	Home Ground, (commonly called the Ferne Ground)	Pasture ...	5	0	11
126	Little Ground	Ditto ...	1	1	27
127	The Meadow	Ditto ...	3	1	19
129	Withy Bed adjoining the Brook	... ...	0	0	13
		TOTAL	A36	1	25

N.B.—*Nos. 208, 210, 211, are now thrown together and form one field.

Land Tax, £7 4s.   Apportioned Tithe Rent Charges, £4 7s. 8d., payable to Vicar of Chisledon. Quit Rents, payable to Lords of the Manor of Badbury, 6s. 6d. and 3s. 2d. per annum.

The Estate lies almost in a ring-fence, and adjoins the Public Highway (late Turnpike Road from Swindon to Hungerford and Marlborough) and Property of the Dean and Chapter of Westminster, and Trustees of the late John Stone, Esq.

The Dwelling-House, with a slight outlay, might be converted into a genteel Family Residence.

Possession will be given on the 11th day of October next.

"I had a pointer that exhibited this faculty in a curious manner. She was weakly when young, and for that reason, together with other circumstances, was never properly trained: a fact that may perhaps have prevented her 'mind' from congealing into the stolidity of routine. She became an outdoor pet, and followed at heel everywhere. One day some ponds were netted, and of the fish taken a few chanced to be placed in a great stone trough from which cattle drank in the yard – a common thing in the country. Some time afterwards, the trough being foul, the fish – they were roach, tench, perch, and one small jack – were removed to a shallow tub while it was being cleansed. In this tub, being scarcely a foot deep though broad, the fish were of course distinctly visible, and at once became an object of the most intense interest to the pointer. She would not leave it; but stood watching every motion of the fish, with her head now on one side now on the other. There she must have remained some hours, and was found at last in the act of removing them one by one and laying them softly, quite unhurt, on the grass.

I put them back into the water, and waited to see the result. She took a good look, and then plunged her nose right under the surface and half-way up the neck completely submerging the head, and in that position groped about on the bottom till a fish came in contact with her mouth and was instantly snatched out. Her head must have been under water each time nearly a minute, feeling for the fish. One by one she drew them out and placed them on the ground, till only the jack remained. He puzzled her, darting away swift as an arrow and seeming to anticipate the enemy. But after a time he, too, was captured. They were not injured – not the mark of a tooth was to be seen – and swam as freely as ever when restored to the water."

The Gamekeeper at Home

"Pan raced beside them after dinner to the ha-ha wall, down which they jumped one after the other into the meadow. The spaniel hesitated on the brink, not that he feared the leap, which he had so often taken, but reflection checked him. He watched them a little way as they ran for the brook, then turned and walked very slowly back to the house; for he knew that now dinner was over, if he waited till he was remembered, a plateful would come out for him."

Bevis: the Story of a Boy

Myriads of Insects

Insects – or rather invertebrates, since the term is used to include arachnids, worms, snails etc. – were ever present in Jefferies' life, both on the farm and in town, and he mentions them often. One phrase he uses many times is "the midsummer hum", to describe "the deep humming sound in the atmosphere above" that insects make. The following phrase from *Field and Hedgerow* gives an idea of the sort of numbers of insects involved: "This forest land is marked by the myriads of insects that roam about it in the days of sunshine. Of all the million million heathbells – multiply them again by a million million more – that purple the acres of rolling hills, mile upon mile, there is not one that is not daily visited by these flying creatures. Countless and incalculable hosts of the yellow-barred hover-flies come to them; the heath and common, the moor and forest, the hedgerow and copse, are full of insects. They rise under foot, they rise from the spray brushed by your arm as you pass, they settle down in front of you – a rain of insects, a coloured shower."

Clearly in Victorian times, insects existed in great abundance. But even back then, Jefferies noticed reductions in numbers, commenting in *Field and Hedgerow*: "This summer, too, there seems a marked absence of bees, butterflies, and other insects in the fields." Such observations were always accompanied by connected thoughts. Seeing fewer insects in his travels, Jefferies looks for reasons by drawing on the interconnected nature of everything in nature, referring to the "interdependence of flowers and insects," and asking: "Is there any connection between the absence of insects and the absence of swallows?"

LEFT: Illustration from the story of the cunning spider, a 'moral' tale within the children's novel Wood Magic.

RIGHT: Beehive at Coate Farm. This type of layered beehive was designed later in the 19th century, by William Broughton Carr.

Insects also provided Jefferies with a few thoughts about flight, particularly the future of human flight. Looking at the flight mechanisms of both birds and bees, the author made several enthusiastic amateur observations relating to the motions of lift and forward propulsion.

Strangely foretelling the tiny drones developed for military use today, Jefferies predicted that craft might be developed following the principles of insect flight. In *The Old House at Coate*, a series of essays published after his death, he writes: "Possibly a motor may be worked out from the insect's wing: possibly it may assist in solving the problems, afford a means of aerial navigation. One difficulty of the navigation is the lack of an engine at once light enough, capable of working on the very little fuel, and at immense speed. The insect answers all these."

Jefferies' thoughts led him to conclude that man would fly one day and, perhaps because of the variety of methods he saw in nature, he said: "I think in all probability several methods of flying will almost simultaneously be discovered."

"Butterfly blue – but there are several varieties; and this plan is interfered with by two things: first, that almost every single item of nature, however minute, has got a distinctly different colour, so that the dictionary of tints would be immense; and next, so very few would know the object itself that the colour attached to it would have no meaning."

Field and Hedgerow

"The yellow butterfly, if you meet one in October, has so toned down his spring yellow that you might fancy him a pale green leaf floating along the road. There is a shining, quivering, gleaming; there is a changing, fluttering, shifting; there is a mixing, weaving – varnished wings, translucent wings, wings with dots and veins, all playing over the purple heath; a very tangle of many-toned lights and hues."

Field and Hedgerow

"A butterfly painted a velvety red with white spots came floating along the surface of the corn, and played round his cap, which was a little higher, and was so tinted by the sun that the butterfly was inclined to settle on it. Guido put up his hand to catch the butterfly, forgetting his secret in his desire to touch it. The butterfly was too quick – with a snap of his wings disdainfully mocking the idea of catching him, away he went."

The Open Air

Victorian Natural History

Since the early nineteenth century, artists such as Constable and Turner, and writers like the Romantic poets, had celebrated the beauty of nature and the countryside. During the Victorian period, advances in communication and publishing made awareness of the natural world greater still and provided a striking contrast to the industrial, urbanised world with its resultant pollution and poverty.

One of the first to capture the imagination of the general public was a young Charles Darwin who, in 1831, joined the crew of the Beagle on a five-year voyage to explore the coastline of South America. These experiences laid the ground work for his seminal 1859 work: *On the Origin of Species*. What Darwin's account of the voyage also did was bring inspirational stories of adventure, exploration and the novelty of faraway lands into Victorian parlours. One of Darwin's admirers was a German doctor and zoologist, Ernest Haeckel, who introduced the word 'ecology' to the public in the mid nineteenth century.

As the century progressed, Britain's geographical horizons expanded overseas through trade and empire. Exploration was a nationalist endeavour designed to map, name and stake a claim on supposedly uninhabited natural spaces around the globe. Nevertheless, expeditions such as that of the Beagle, and of David Livingstone into the African interior, often took with them naturalists who brought back specimens. By the mid nineteenth century these needed a permanent home where the Victorian public and scientists could study them. Previously, museums had been the preserve of the rich, but a visionary called Richard Owen declared that a new museum should be built as a cathedral to nature, with free access for all. Accordingly, part of the proceeds from the 1851 Great Exhibition went towards the cost of building the new Natural History Museum in Kensington, London, which opened in 1881.

In the latter half of the nineteenth century, a growing minority of Victorians, like Jefferies, began to question the relationship between humans and nature and look for ways in which to restore a balance which humans and industrialisation had interfered with. In Ruskin's 1884 *The Storm-Cloud of the Nineteenth Century*, the threat to nature comes from human action, such as the rise in air pollution, and can be viewed as a nascent exposé of climate change. At the same time, some individuals actively lobbied to preserve nature. Alfred Newton, a Cambridge professor and passionate ornithologist was instrumental in canvassing public opinion to protect birds, leading to the introduction of the closed season. Building on the rising tide of belief in the value and importance of nature, the National Trust was founded in 1895. One of the founders, Octavia Hill, wrote that part of her rationale for setting up the Trust was because 'We all want quiet. We all want beauty ... we all need space. Unless we have it, we cannot reach that sense of quiet in which whispers of better things come to us gently.'

"Once upon a time there was a very cunning spider – a very cunning spider indeed. The old toad by the rhubarb told Bevis there had not been such a cunning spider for many summers; he knew almost as much about flies as the old toad, and caught such a great number, that the toad began to think there would be none left for him. Now the toad was extremely fond of flies, and he watched the spider with envy, and grew more angry about it every day.

As he sat blinking and winking by the rhubarb in his house all day long, the toad never left off thinking, thinking, thinking about the spider. And as he kept thinking, thinking, thinking, so he told Bevis, he recollected that he knew a great deal about a good many other things besides flies. So one day, after several weeks of thinking, he crawled out of his house in the sunshine, which he did not like at all, and went across the grass to the iron railings, where the spider had then got his web. The spider saw him coming, and being very proud of his cleverness, began to taunt and tease him.

'Your back is all over warts, and you are an old toad,' he said. 'You are so old, that I heard the swallows saying their great-great-great-grandmothers, when they built in the chimney, did not know when you were born. And you have got foolish, and past doing anything, and so stupid that you hardly know when it is going to rain. Why, the sun is shining bright, you stupid old toad, and there isn't a chance of a single drop falling. You look very ugly down there in the grass. Now, don't you wish that you were me and could catch more flies than you could eat? Why, I can catch wasps and bees, and tie them up so tight with my threads that they cannot sting nor even move their wings, nor so much as wriggle their bodies. I am the very cleverest and most cunning spider that ever lived.'"

Wood Magic

"The heavy humble-bee is generally seen close to the earth, and often goes down into the depths of the dry ditches, and may there be heard buzzing slowly along under the arch of briar and bramble. He seems to lose his way now and then in the tangled undergrowth of the woods; and if a footstep disturbs and alarms him, it is amusing to see his desperate efforts to free himself hastily from the interlacing grass-blades and ferns."

The Gamekeeper at Home

"The number of wasp-flies, or Hoverers, in this healthy district is extraordinary. Every spot is visited by them. If I stay a moment while walking up the hill, I see them at the heath on the bank. If I watch the hedge as I walk on I see several at every step hanging on the air in their peculiar manner wherever there is foliage or grass, examining everything. In the garden nineteen come in five minutes to a standard rose.

I have seen a small wasp-fly actually alight on the back of a humble-bee that was sucking a white clover bloom. The weight of the fly upset the humble-bee which fell on the sward, got up and flew away without taking further notice."

Chronicle of the Hedges

121

"There were cottagers in this lonely hill hamlet, not only old folk but young persons, who had never seen a train. They had not had the enterprise or curiosity to walk into Overboro for the purpose. Some of the folk ate snails, the common brown shell-snail found in the hedges. It has been observed that children who eat snails are often remarkably plump. The method of cooking is to place the snail in its shell on the bar of a grate, like a chestnut. And well-educated people have been known, even in these days, to use the snail as an external medicine for weakly children: rubbed into the back or limb, the substance of the snail is believed to possess strengthening virtues."

Round About a Great Estate

"On the wings of the dragon-fly as he hovers an instant before he darts there is a prismatic gleam. These wing textures are even more delicate than the minute filaments on a swallow's quill, more delicate than the pollen of a flower. They are formed of matter indeed, but how exquisitely it is resolved into the means and organs of life!"

The Life of the Fields

Boughs of a Tree

Trees, and their smaller cousins, shrubs and bushes, dominated much of the landscape in Jefferies' world, particularly out in the country, but also in the parks and gardens of more urban areas. Although much of Wiltshire is made up of 'the Plain', as well as rolling hills and downs, the author didn't have any shortage of access to green foliage at Coate, with a garden full of trees, copses and hedges breaking up the agricultural landscape, and full-on forests, like Savernake, within walking distance.

Even when the family moved to Surbiton so Jefferies could be nearer to London and its publishing opportunities, the new home they rented was situated next to thick woods, giving the house its address of 2, Woodside. The name could not have been more appropriate for a lover of nature. The area still boasts old oak trees, a large green oasis and the *Richard Jefferies Bird Sanctuary*. However, one of Jefferies' disappointments of urban life was the use of foreign varieties of trees, with blandly uniform gardens full of "acacias, sumachs, cedar deodaras, araucarias, laurels, planes, beds of rhododendrons, and so on." To someone like Jefferies, used to exploring the much more natural English countryside, this was a "a pitiful spectacle." Where, he asks, are the sycamores, limes, horse-chestnuts, hawthorns and birches? Why does no-one plant young ash trees, or enjoy the red, green and yellow of the elm? Most importantly, why would you choose trees like the plane or the laurel: "How tame and insignificant are these compared with the oak! Thrice a year the oaks become beautiful in a different way. In spring the opening buds give the tree a ruddy hue; in summer the great head of green is not to be surpassed; in autumn, with the falling leaf and acorn, they appear buff and brown. The nobility of the oak casts the pitiful laurel into utter insignificance."

Two trees from Jefferies' childhood get special mention: at Coate Water, the 'Council Oak' features in *Bevis*, where a large group of children convene before a mock battle between Caesar and Pompey; and, in the garden of Coate Farm, a large mulberry tree was planted by Jefferies' grandfather in the 1830s, and called 'The Tree of Life' in a rare offering of poetry by his author grandson.

LEFT: Sign for 'The Council Oak', at Coate Water.

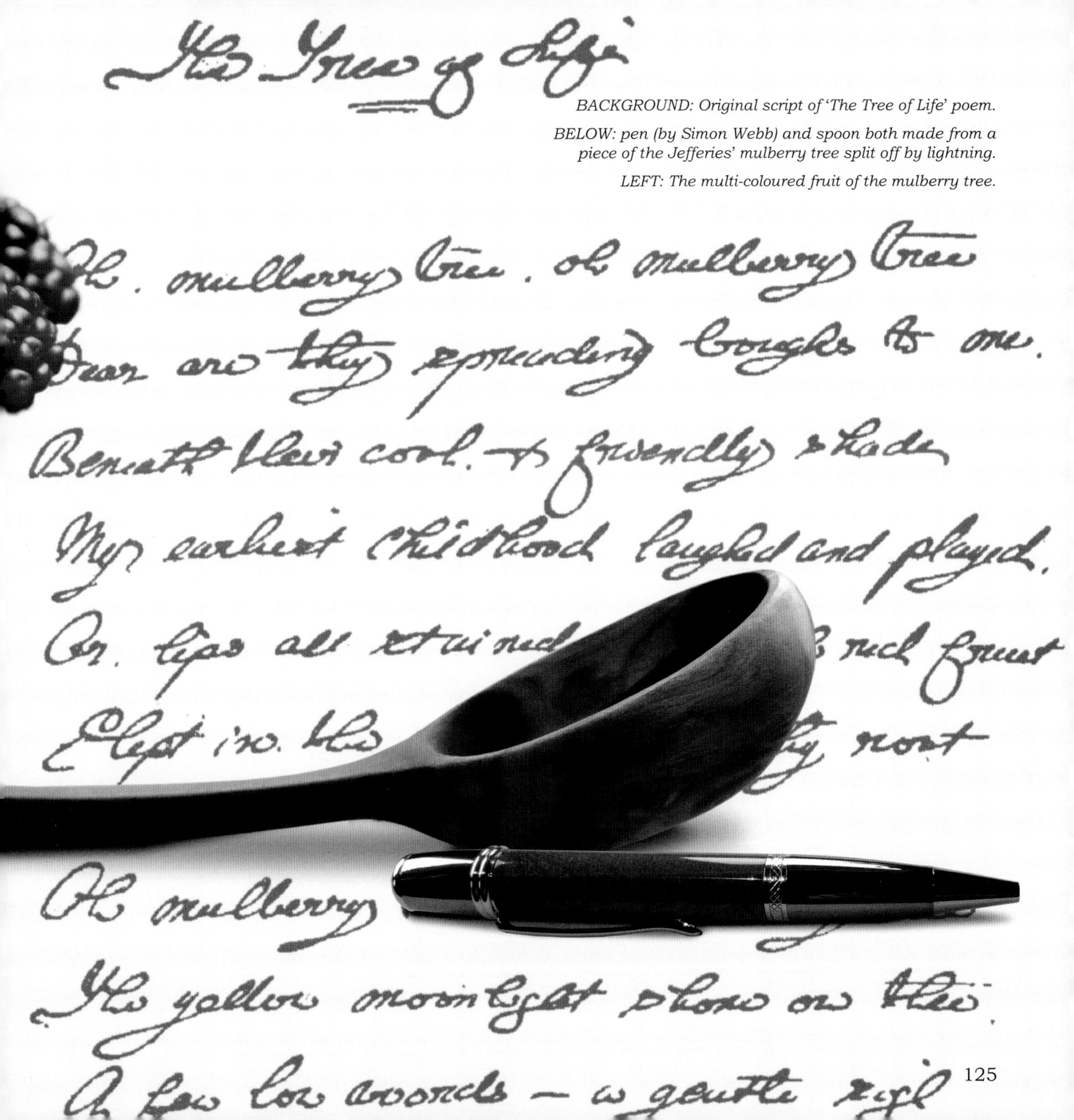

The Tree of Life
Oh. mulberry tree. oh mulberry tree
Dear are thy spreading boughs to me.
Beneath their cool & friendly shade
My earliest Childhood laughed and played.
On lips all stained
rich fruit
root
Oh mulberry
The yellow moonlight shone on thee.
A few low words – a gentle sigh

BACKGROUND: Original script of 'The Tree of Life' poem.

BELOW: pen (by Simon Webb) and spoon both made from a piece of the Jefferies' mulberry tree split off by lightning.

LEFT: The multi-coloured fruit of the mulberry tree.

"Oh, mulberry tree, oh mulberry tree
          Dear are thy spreading boughs to me.
          Beneath their cool and friendly shade
My earliest childhood laughed and played.
Or, lips all stained with rich red fruit
Slept in the long grass at thy root.

Oh mulberry tree, oh mulberry tree !
The yellow moonlight shone on thee.
A few low words – a gentle sigh,
A tear within the upturned eye.
"I love – my fate to thee resign" –
A nameless thrill, and she was mine.

The mid-day sun in splendour blazed,
And all who stood around me praised.
The deed was done, the fame went round,
My brows with laurel leaves were crowned
My first – my proudest victory
Beneath thy boughs, oh mulberry tree.

The tears of Heaven were falling fast,
Mourning the memory of the past.
I knelt beneath the broken limb
In rain and night, and wept for him.
I saw the tomb – the planks laid there,
To slide the coffin to its lair,
"Ashes to ashes", this the end,
My first, my last – my only friend!

The morning stars grew pale and few,
In chilly draughts the east wind blew,
Lifting the black and frost-strewn leaves
In rustling eddies to the eaves.
Deceived no more with life's vain lies,
And all things equal in mine eyes,
I wait still near the mulberry tree
The dawning of eternity.

Whoe'er shall pluck the mulberry tree,
Bitter and sweet its fruit shall be;
Such – joy and misery still at strife –
The berries of the Tree of Life."

The Mulberry Tree

The mulberry tree (centre) at Richard Jefferies' birthplace, Coate Farm.

"The snow on the ground increases the sense of light, and in approaching the wood the scene is even more distinct than during the gloomy day. The tips of the short stubble that has not yet been ploughed in places just protrude above the surface, and the snow, frozen hard, crunches with a low sound under foot. But for that all is perfectly still. The level upland cornfields stretch away white and vacant to the hills – white, too, and clear against the sky. The plain is silent, and nothing that can be seen moves upon its surface.

On the verge of the wood which occupies the sloping ground there stands a great oak tree, and down one side of its trunk is a narrow white streak of snow. Leaning against the oak and looking upwards, every branch and twig is visible, lit up by the moon. Overhead the stars are dimmed, but they shine more brightly yonder above the hills. Such leaves as have not yet fallen hang motionless: those that are lying on the ground are covered by the snow, and thus held fast from rustling even were the wind to blow. But there is not the least breath--a great frost is always quiet, profoundly quiet – and the silence is undisturbed even by the fall of a leaf. The frost that kills them holds the leaves till it melts, and then they drop.

The tall ash poles behind in the wood stand stark and straight, pointing upwards, and it is possible to see for some distance between them. No lesser bats flit to and fro outside the fence under the branches; no larger ones pass above the tops of the trees. There seems, indeed, a total absence of life. The pheasants are at roost in the warmer covers; and the woodpigeons are also perched – some in the detached oaks of the hedgerows, particularly those that are thickly grown with ivy about the upper branches. Up in the great beeches the rooks are still and silent; sometimes the boughs are encrusted with rime about their very claws."

The Amateur Poacher

"The hawthorn is a part of natural English life – country life. It stands side by side with the Englishman, as the palm tree is pictured side by side with the Arab. You cannot pick up an old play, or book of the time when old English life was in the prime, without finding some reference to the hawthorn. There is nothing of this in the laurel, or any shrub whatever that may be thrust in with a ticket to tell you its name; it has a ticket because it has no interest, or else you would know it.

For use there is nothing like hawthorn; it will trim into a thick hedge, defending the enclosure from trespassers, and warding off the bitter winds; or it will grow into a tree. Again, the old hedge-crab – the common, despised crab-apple – in spring is covered with blossom, such a mass of blossom that it may be distinguished a mile. Did any one ever see a plane or a laurel look like that?

Nature Near London

"There is a part of the wood where the bushes grow but thinly and the ash-stoles are scattered at some distance from each other. It is on a steep slope – almost cliff – where the white chalk comes to the surface. On the edge above rise tall beech trees with smooth round trunks, whose roots push and project through the wall of chalk, and bend downwards, sometimes dislodging lumps of rubble to roll headlong among the bushes below. A few small firs cling half-way up, and a tangled, matted mass of briar and bramble climbs nearly to them, with many a stout thistle flourishing vigorously.

The Gamekeeper at Home

"Besides the elms there is a noble avenue of limes, and great oaks scattered here and there, under whose ample shade the cattle repose in the heat of the day.

In summer from out the leafy chambers of the limes there falls the pleasant sound of bees innumerable, the voice of whose trembling wings lulls the listening ear as the drowsy sunshine weighs the eyelid till I walk the avenue in a dream. It leads out into the park – no formal gravel drive, simply a footpath on the sward between the flowering trees: a path that becomes less and less marked as I advance, and finally fades away, where the limes cease, in the broad level of the opening 'greeny field.' These honey-bees seem to fly higher and to exhibit much more activity than the great humble-bee: here in the limes they must be thirty feet above the ground."

The Gamekeeper at Home

"When the hedgers and ditchers were put to work to cut a hedge – the turn of every hedge comes round once in so many years – they used to be instructed, if they came across a sapling oak, ash, or elm, to spare it, and cut away the bushes to give it full play. But now they chop and slash away without remorse, and the young forest-tree rising up with a promise of future beauty falls before the billhook. In time the full-grown oaks and elms of the hedgerow decay, or are felled; and in consequence of this careless destruction of the saplings there is nothing to fill their place. The charm of English meadows consisted in no small degree in the stately trees, whose shadows lengthened with the declining sun and gave such pleasant shelter from the heat. Soon, however, if the rising generation of trees is thus cut down, they must become bare, open, and unlovely."

The Amateur Poacher

LEFT: tree management at Coate Water.

One side of the summer-house was a thick holly-bush, Iden had set it there; he builded the summer-house and set the ivy; and the pippin at the back, whose bloom was white; the copper-birch near by; the great sycamore alone had been there before him, but he set a seat under it, and got woodbine to flower there; the drooping-ash he planted, and if Amaryllis stood under it when the tree was in full leaf you could not see her, it made so complete an arbour; the Spanish oak in the corner; the box hedge along the ha-ha parapet; the red currants against the red wall; the big peony yonder; the damsons and pear; the yellow honey-bush; all these, and this was but one square, one mosaic of the garden, half of it sward, too, and besides these there was the rhubarb-patch at one corner; fruit, flowers, plants, and herbs, lavender, parsley, which has a very pleasant green, growing in a thick bunch, roses, pale sage – read Boccaccio and the sad story of the leaf of sage – ask Nature if you wish to know how many things more there were."

Amaryllis at the Fair

The apple was the apple of fruit, the natural medicine of man – and the best flavoured. It was compounded of the sweetest extracts and essences of air and light, put together of sunshine and wind and shower in such a way that no laboratory could imitate: and so on in a strain and with a simplicity of language that reminded you of Bacon and his philosophy of the Elizabethan age.

Iden in a way certainly had a tinge of the Baconian culture, naturally, and not from any study of that author, whose books he had never seen. The great Bacon was, in fact, a man of orchard and garden, and gathered his ideas from the fields.

Just look at an apple on the tree, said Iden. Look at a Blenheim orange, the inimitable mixture of colour, the gold and bronze, and ruddy tints, not bright colours – undertones of bright colours – smoothed together and polished, and made the more delightful by occasional roughness in the rind. Or look at the brilliant King Pippin. Now he was getting older he found, however, that the finest of them all was the russet. For eating, at its proper season, it was good, but for cooking it was simply the Imperial Cæsar and Sultan of apples; whether for baking, or pies, or sauce, there was none to equal it. Apple-sauce made of the real true russet was a sauce for Jove's own table. It was necessary that it should be the real russet. Indeed in apple trees you had to be as careful of breeding and pedigree as the owners of racing stables were about their horses."

Amaryllis at the Fair

136

"But the sun gets low. Following this broad green drive, it leads us past vistas of endless glades, going no man knows where, into shadow and gloom; past grand old oaks; past places where the edge of a veritable wilderness comes up to the trees – a wilderness of gnarled hawthorn trunks of unknown ages, of holly with shining metallic-green leaves, and hazel-bushes.

Past tall trees bearing the edible chestnut in prickly clusters; past maples which in a little while will be painted in crimson and gold, with the deer peeping out of the fern everywhere, and once, perhaps, catching a glimpse of a shy, beautiful, milk-white doe. Past a huge hollow trunk in the midst of a greensward, where merry picnic parties under the 'King Oak' tread the social quadrille, or whirl waltzes to the harp and flute. For there are certain spots even in this grand solitude consecrated to Cytherea and Bacchus, as he is now worshipped in champagne. And where can graceful forms look finer, happy eyes more bright, than in this natural ballroom, under its incomparable roof of blue, supported upon living columns of stately trees?

Still onward, into a gravel carriage-road now, returning by degrees to civilization, and here, with happy judgment, the hand of man has aided Nature. Far as the eye can see extends an avenue of beech, passing right through the forest. The tall, smooth trunks rise up to a great height, and then branch overhead, looking like the roof of a Gothic cathedral. The growth is so regular and so perfect that the comparison springs unbidden to the lip, and here, if anywhere, that order of architecture might have taken its inspiration. There is a continuous Gothic arch of green for miles, beneath which one may drive or walk, as in the aisles of a forest abbey. But it is impossible to even mention all the beauties of this place within so short a space. It must suffice to say that the visitor may walk for whole days in this great wood, and never pass the same spot twice. No gates or jealous walls will bar his progress. As the fancy seizes him, so he may wander."

Marlborough Forest

LEFT: One of the ancient oaks in the Savernake, the Big-Bellied Oak.

Built of Wood

The love of trees in their natural environment was not Jefferies' only relationship with them, he also loved wood. Wood in the nineteenth century was still very much the major material for producing goods: buildings, furniture, vehicles, toys, and even the tools to make them all.

In *Bevis*, Jefferies tells us that there were at least two places for working with wood on the farm: "He went up into the bench-room where there was another carpenter's bench (put up for amateur work)." We know that he made a tiny wooden 'chest of drawers' when he was a young boy, and his writing suggests that carpentry was a fairly regular hobby. Again, in *Bevis*, he describes making the wooden stock for a gun, building a raft out of a packing case, and "Once, too, he took the gouge and the largest chisel from the workshop, and the mallet with the beech-wood head, and set to work to dig out a boat from a vast trunk of elm thrown long since, and lying outside the rick-yard, whither it had been drawn under the timber-carriage."

The theme of primitive woodworking, taking a tree at its most fundamental and making use of it – in this case as a dug-out canoe – occurs again in *After London*: "On the bank Felix had found a fine black poplar, the largest and straightest and best grown of that sort for some distance round, and this he had selected for his canoe. He had chosen the black poplar for the canoe because it was the lightest wood, and would float best. To fell so large a tree had been a great labour, for the axes were of poor quality, cut badly, and often required sharpening. He could easily have ordered half-a-dozen men to throw the tree, and they would have obeyed immediately; but then the individuality and interest of the work would have been lost. Unless he did it himself its importance and value to him would have been diminished. It had now been down some weeks, had been hewn into outward shape, and the larger part of the interior slowly dug away with chisel and gouge."

Perhaps unsurprisingly, given how pervasive wooden items were in his day, Jefferies refers to working with wood, or makes comment about wooden items, many times in his work. But, like so many other aspects of his life, even wood provided a source of conflict in the writer's mind. There was no problem between loving the live trees and their use as a material provider, that was simply a good all round relationship. The conflict for Jefferies related to ambiguity over his love of the past versus the inevitable consequences of progress. For example, in his agricultural essays Jefferies gives much advice about the need for modernisation, suggesting that old butter-making practice, and its wooden apparatus, should be replaced with modern techniques and equipment. At the same time, he mourns the replacement of wooden items with iron, and the knock-on effect this has on the countryside:

"Hedge-carpentering was, in fact, a distinct business, followed by one or two men in every locality; but iron now supplants everything, and the hedges themselves are disappearing."

The Gamekeeper at Home

OPPOSITE: Tiny wooden two-drawer cabinet which Jefferies made as a boy.

BELOW: Double-handed saw for tree felling, and adze for chopping wood at a different angle from a standard axe.

I den's flag-basket of tools lay by the gate, it was a new gate, and he had been fitting it before he went in to lunch. His basket was of flag because the substance of the flag is soft, and the tools, chisels, and so on, laid pleasant in it; he must have everything right. The new gate was of solid oak, no "sappy" stuff, real heart of oak, well-seasoned, without a split, fine, close-grained timber, cut on the farm, and kept till it was thoroughly fit, genuine English oak. If you would only consider Iden's gate you might see there the man."

Amaryllis at the Fair

L et not the modern Goths destroy our hedges, so typical of an English landscape, so full of all that can delight the eye and please the mind. Spare them, if only for the sake of the 'days when we went gipsying – a long time ago'; spare them for the children to gather the flowers of May and the blackberries of September."

The Hills and Vales

Flowers Shone Forth

Jefferies's love of flowers, wild flowers in particular, surpassed just about everything else. In his mind, as people grow older everything else loses its romance and fades – "wild flowers alone never become commonplace." And his capacity for finding wild flowers, and knowing all their names, was astonishing. Take the following single sentence from his essay *Nature Near London:* "There are about sixty wild flowers which grow freely along this road, namely, yellow agrimony, amphibious persicaria, arum, avens, bindweed, bird's foot lotus, bittersweet, blackberry, black and white bryony, brooklime, burdock, buttercups, wild camomile, wild carrot, celandine (the great and lesser), cinquefoil, cleavers, corn buttercup, corn mint, corn sowthistle, and spurrey, cowslip, cow-parsnip, wild parsley, daisy, dandelion, dead nettle, and white dog rose, and trailing rose, violets (the sweet and the scentless), figwort, veronica,

ground ivy, willowherb (two sorts), herb Robert, honeysuckle, lady's smock, purple loosestrife, mallow, meadow-orchis, meadow-sweet, yarrow, moon daisy, St. John's wort, pimpernel, water plantain, poppy, rattles, scabious, self-heal, silverweed, sowthistle, stitchwort, teazles, tormentil, vetches, and yellow vetch." Perhaps what is most startling about this list, is that such abundance was normal in Victorian times. The verges around his birthplace today are dominated with grass and nettles; he would be hard pushed to find even small clusters of wild flower varieties.

In his 1875 novel *Restless Human Hearts*, Jefferies talks about the importance of the history of flowers, almost dismissing some highly

cultivated garden varieties for their newness. He felt the wild varieties we all know and love hold all the more depth because of the associations they build up over time, with connections and memories of our own lives. Jefferies was interested in the "soul of the flowers." He wondered what was going on inside each flower and was fascinated by the language barrier between us and them, while appreciating the strength of feeling they can still evoke. He expresses it best in this quote from *The Open Air*: "Before I had any conscious thought it was a delight to me to find wild flowers, just to see them. Without conscious thought of seasons and the advancing hours to light on the white wild violet, the meadow orchis, the blue veronica, the blue meadow cranesbill; feeling the warmth and delight of the increasing sun-rays, but not recognising whence or why it was joy."

As well as the more obvious blooms, Jefferies was just as interested in every other sort of flora: the grasses, climbers and parasites; herbs like lavender, sweet marjoram, rosemary, rue, bay, thyme, and "some pot-herbs whose use is forgotten;" mushrooms, toadstools, lichens and mosses; and everything else that grows up from the fields, verges, roads and ditches.

LEFT: *Sketches of wild flowers, from one of Jefferies' many notebooks.*

OPPOSITE: *Bluebells in Hodson Woods, painted by Kate Tryon.*

ABOVE: *Drawing by Jefferies, of an anenome leaf.*

143

appily this park escaped, and it is beautiful. Our English landscape wants no gardening: it cannot be gardened. The least interference kills it. The beauty of English woodland and country is in its detail. There is nothing empty and unclothed. If the clods are left a little while undisturbed in the fields, weeds spring up and wild-flowers bloom upon them. Is the hedge cut and trimmed, lo! the bluebells flower the more and a yet fresher green buds forth upon the twigs. Never was there a garden like the meadow: there is not an inch of the meadow in early summer without a flower."

Field and Hedgerow

"Without conscious thought of seasons and the advancing hours to light on the white wild violet, the meadow orchis, the blue veronica, the blue meadow cranesbill; feeling the warmth and delight of the increasing sun-rays, but not recognising whence or why it was joy. All the world is young to a boy, and thought has not entered into it; even the old men with grey hair do not seem old; different but not aged, the idea of age has not been mastered."

The Open Air

"Mrs. Iden was very fond of lavender, the scent, and the plant in every form. She kept little bags of it in all her drawers, and everything at Coombe Oaks upstairs in the bedrooms had a faint, delicious lavender perfume. There is nothing else that smells so sweet and clean and dry. You cannot imagine a damp sheet smelling of lavender. Iden himself liked lavender, and used to rub it between his finger and thumb in the garden, as he did, too, with the black-currant leaves and walnut-leaves, if he fancied anything he had touched might have left an unpleasant odour adhering to his skin. He said it cleaned his hands as much as washing them. Iden liked Mrs. Iden to like lavender because his mother had been so fond of it, and all the sixteen carved oak-presses which had been so familiar to him in boyhood were full of a thick atmosphere of the plant. Long since, while yet the honeymoon bouquet remained in the wine of life, Iden had set a hedge of lavender to please his wife. It was so carefully chosen, and set, and watched, that it grew to be the finest lavender in all the country. People used to come for it from round about, quite certain of a favourable reception, for there was nothing so sure to bring peace at Coombe Oaks as a mention of lavender."

Amaryllis at the Fair

"The kingly poppies on the dry summit of the mound take no heed of these, the populace, their subjects so numerous they cannot be numbered. A barren race they are, the proud poppies, lords of the July field, taking no deep root, but raising up a brilliant blazon of scarlet heraldry out of nothing. They are useless, they are bitter, they are allied to sleep and poison and everlasting night; yet they are forgiven because they are not commonplace. Nothing, no abundance of them, can ever make the poppies commonplace. There is genius in them, the genius of colour, and they are saved. Even when they take the room of the corn we must admire them. The mighty multitude of nations, the millions and millions of the grass stretching away in intertangled ranks, through pasture and mead from shore to shore, have no kinship with these their lords."

Field and Hedgerow

"There had been daffodils in that spot at least a century, opening every March to the dry winds that shrivel up the brown dead leaves of winter, and carry them out from the bushes under the trees, sending them across the meadow – fleeing like a routed army before the bayonets of the East. Every spring for a century at least the daffodils had bloomed there."

Amaryllis at the Fair

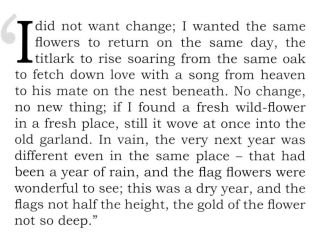

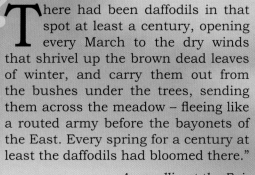

"I did not want change; I wanted the same flowers to return on the same day, the titlark to rise soaring from the same oak to fetch down love with a song from heaven to his mate on the nest beneath. No change, no new thing; if I found a fresh wild-flower in a fresh place, still it wove at once into the old garland. In vain, the very next year was different even in the same place – that had been a year of rain, and the flag flowers were wonderful to see; this was a dry year, and the flags not half the height, the gold of the flower not so deep."

The Open Air

"There are a million books, and yet with all their aid I cannot tell you the colour of the May dandelion. There are three greens at this moment in my mind: that of the leaf of the flower-de-luce, that of the yellow iris leaf, and that of the bayonet-like leaf of the common flag. With admission to a million books, how am I to tell you the difference between these tints? So many, many books, and such a very, very little bit of nature in them! Though we have been so many thousand years upon the earth we do not seem to have done any more as yet than walk along beaten footpaths, and sometimes really it would seem as if there were something in the minds of many men quite artificial, quite distinct from the sun and trees and hills – altogether house people, whose gods must be set in four-cornered buildings. There is nothing in books that touches my dandelion."

Field and Hedgerow

"A few scattered firs, the remnants of extinct plantations, grew on the slope, and green 'fairy rings' marked it here and there. These fairy rings have a somewhat different appearance from the dark green semicircles found in the meadows and called by the same name: the latter are often only segments of circles, are found near hedges, and almost always either under a tree or where a tree has been. There were more mushrooms on the side of the hill than we cared to carry. Some eat mushrooms raw – fresh as taken from the ground, with a little salt: to me the taste is then too strong. Of the many ways of cooking them the simplest is the best; that is, on a gridiron over wood embers on the hearth."

The Hills and Vales

"Here also may be found the wild garlic, which sometimes gets among the wheat and lends an onion-like flavour to the bread. It grows, too, on the edge of the low chalky banks overhanging the narrow waggon-track, whose ruts are deep in the rubble – worn so in winter."

Wild Life in a Southern County

BACKGROUND: *Photograph of Jefferies aged 33.*

152

People

Talking of People

Jefferies is most often thought of as a 'nature writer'. He has been described as 'the prose-poet of the English landscape', 'a pioneer environmentalist', 'the Wiltshire naturalist', 'the least conventional of nineteenth-century observers of the natural world', 'a landscape painter in words', and 'the first and truest nature conservationist.' While all these epitaphs are fitting, they don't tell the whole story. Take another look at the titles of some of his books: *The Gamekeeper at Home, The Amateur Poacher, Hodge and His Masters, Bevis: the Story of a Boy, Amaryllis at the Fair, The Rise of Maximin, The Toilers in the Field,* and *Ben Tubbs' Adventures.* Each of these titles refers to a person, or people, as does *The Story of My Heart: An Autobiography.* And the novels – *The Dewy Morn, Restless Human Hearts, After London, Greene Ferne Farm,* and *The Scarlet Shawl* – none of these shout out as purely 'nature' books either.

Jefferies was as interested in the human condition as he was in anything else; he was fascinated by nature, of course, but also by our relationship with it – with *our* habitat. It is in many ways what set him apart from other writers of his time and for a long time after him, and why he can be seen as a true ecologist, not only of other species but also of our own, human, species.

Given Jefferies' career in writing about agriculture and his passion for the countryside, it was inevitable that most of his observations about people were in this context. However, it was not exclusively so. In his short lifetime the writer mixed in different levels of society, visited different places, experienced different relationships, and lived through different degrees of human success and failure. His writing covers all these things, from the crowds of London and the "belles who flourish in Belgravia," to the sophisticated charcoal-using Parisians and "the eyes of the wounded in the ambulance-waggons that came pouring into Brussels after Sudan." His thoughts stretch from an idealized "child of nature," to a bleak, greed-fuelled end to civilization, and take in everyone from avaricious monks and scary doctors, to great architects and the Aldboume bell-founder who "worked as truly, and in as careful a manner, as if he had known his bell was to be hung in St. Peter's at Rome."

LEFT: Set of 'latten' or horse team bells, cast in Aldbourne, Wiltshire.

"There is one long street, just as would be found in the far west, with fields at each end. But through this long street, and on and out into the open, is continually pouring the human living undergrowth of that vast forest of life, London."

The Open Air

155

"Amaryllis knew the path perfectly, but if she had not, the tom-tomming of drums and blowing of brass, audible two miles away, would have guided her safely to the fair. The noise became prodigious as she approached – the ceaseless tomtom, the beating of drums and gongs outside the show vans, the shouting of the showmen, the roar of a great crowd, the booing of cattle, the baaing of sheep, the neighing of horses – altogether the "rucket" was tremendous.

She looked back from the hill close to the town and saw the people hurrying in from every quarter – there was a string of them following the path she had come, and others getting over distant stiles. A shower had fallen in the night, but the ceaseless wheels had ground up the dust again, and the lines of the various roads were distinctly marked by the clouds hanging above them. For one on business, fifty hastened on to join the uproar.

Suppose the Venus de Medici had been fetched from Florence and had been set up in the town of Woolhorton, or the Laocoon from Rome, or the Milo from Paris, do you think all these people would have scurried in such haste to admire these beautiful works? Nothing of the sort; if you want a crowd you must make a row. It is really wonderful how people do thoroughly and unaffectedly enjoy a fearful disturbance; if the cannon could be shot off quietly, and guns made no noise, battles would not be half so popular to read about. The silent arrow is uninteresting, and if you describe a mediæval scramble you must put in plenty of splintering lances, resounding armour, shrieks and groans, and so render it lively.

"This is the patent age of new inventions," and some one might make a profit by starting a fête announcing that a drum or a gong would be provided for every individual, to be beaten in a grand universal chorus."

Amaryllis at the Fair

People from the Land

Ever since his letters to *The Times* in 1872, much of what Jefferies wrote about people was from the perspective of the 'farmer class'. And the politics behind the writing reflects this, with deference to land owners and not much thought for lowly labourers. These conservative and often dismissive views were to change as Jefferies went into the 1880s. His writings revealed frustration with what he saw as injustices, and demonstrated an increased empathy towards the suffering of fellow humans, especially those on the poorer side of the class/financial scales.

In 1880, a series of articles for *The Standard* was published in book form as *Hodge and His Masters*. The book presents a collection of diverse caricatures, all in scenes depicting the huge changes taking place in agriculture at the time – the name *Hodge* is a semi-derogatory term used for any country labourer, the Victorian equivalent of today's country bumpkin. The book is still written heavily in defence of the 'lot' of the farmer, but it reveals a significant shift: more cynicism towards the land-owning ruling classes and political power, and more understanding and support for the workers of the soil and the poor in general.

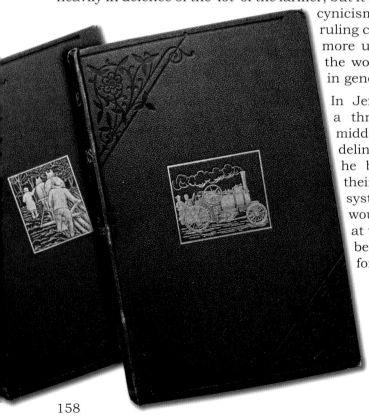

In Jefferies' times, Britain lived in a three-class system, with upper, middle and lower class very clearly delineated. As the author got older he began to realise that, despite their promise, technological and systemic changes in agriculture would rarely benefit the workers at the bottom of the stack, instead being focused on profit margins for the wealthy landowners.

LEFT: The two-part edition of 'Hodge and His Masters', with engravings on the covers illustrating the old and the new worlds of agriculture.

RIGHT: Nineteenth century agricultural labourers.

159

"Had he looked over the hedge in the evening, he might have seen a row of reapers walking down the road at the sudden sound of a jingling bell behind them, open their line, and wheel like a squad, part to the right and part to the left, to let the bicycle pass. After it had gone by they closed their rank, and trudged on toward the village. They had been at work all day in the uplands among the corn, cutting away with their hooks low down the yellow straw. They began in the early morning, and had first to walk two miles or more up to the harvest field. Stooping, as they worked, to strike low enough, the hot sun poured his fierce rays upon their shoulders and the backs of their necks. The sinews of the right arm had continually to drive the steel through straw and tough weeds entangled in the wheat. There was no shadow to sit under for luncheon, save that at the side of the shocks, where the sheaves radiated heat and interrupted the light air, so that the shadow was warmer than the sunshine. Coarse cold bacon and bread, cheese, and a jar of small beer, or a tin can of weak cold tea, were all they had to supply them with fresh strength for further labour.

At last the evening came, the jackets so long thrown aside were resumed, and the walk home began. After so many hours of wearisome labour it was hardly strange that their natural senses were dulled – that they did not look about them, nor converse gaily. By mutual, if unexpressed consent, they intended to call at the wayside inn when they reached it, to rest on the hard bench outside, and take a quart of stronger ale. Thus trudging homewards after that exhausting day, they did not hear the almost silent approach of the bicycle behind till the rider rang his bell."

Hodge and His Masters

LEFT: 'Tin can' flask for non-alcoholic drinks, to clip onto a worker's belt.

Never Meddle with Politics

Jefferies' views on people started from the beginning, in his own childhood. Agricultural and nature articles were a mainstay in the early 1880s, but the publication of *Wood Magic (*1881) and then *Bevis: the Story of a Boy* (1882) broke the author out of his own career mould, giving him some success in fiction, and taking him back to an idealised version of childhood at Coate.

The two books revolve around nature, set in the garden at Coate Farm and around Coate Water but unlike most of Jefferies' work, they depict the world through the eyes of a person: in both cases, Jefferies himself, albeit in a fictionalized form. *Bevis* offers wonderful descriptions of the local countryside, but is actually a story of boyhood and growing up, with all the adventures and some of the tribulations which that involves. In *Wood Magic*, a younger Bevis character converses with all aspects of nature, whether it be animal, bird, tree or wind, and the story is set in the natural world (mainly the gardens at Coate Farm). However, behind the idyllic veneer, the young boy is essentially watching a complex human story unfold. The creatures, dominated by an evil despot and a war-mongering greedy neighbour, present all the machinations of human politics, fear, deceit and power games that make

BELOW: Covers of 'Wood Magic' and 'Bevis'.

162

up the darker underbelly of a fragile society. The characters who Bevis talks to, from the heart-broken mouse whose family has been eaten by the weasel, to the wise and all-seeing wind, are all anthropomorphised – human – as are the scenes which they act out. Jefferies has gone back to his roots, and what must have been a lonely childhood, to think through his views on the politics of life, but within the relative security of harmless children's books.

The books were precursors to the more blatant views that were to follow.

Down in the South

Around the time *Wood Magic* and *Bevis* were published, Jefferies fell ill. For a year, from December 1881, the author was to suffer from the pain and distress of an ailment called fistula, almost certainly connected to tuberculosis. At the time the only hope was to undergo an operation which, in the nineteenth century, would have been very different to having surgery today. The treatment would have been risky and extremely painful, and Jefferies had to undergo the operation four times before doctors managed to get the symptoms in check. Although he wouldn't have been aware of it, the 'disease' was probably connected to the illnesses he suffered when he was younger, and it would go on to kill him in just a few more years.

Like many Victorians, Jefferies believed that the answer to health problems such as those he was experiencing was to be in a different environment, and that generally meant the seaside. As he put it, when writing about Beachy Head: "There is the sea below to bathe in, the air of the sky up hither to breathe, the sun to infuse the invisible magnetism of his beams. These are the three potent medicines of nature, and they are medicines that by degrees strengthen not only the body but the unquiet mind."

So, in 1882, the Jefferies family moved away from Surbiton and into a rented four-storey house in Hove, on the coast alongside Brighton. The house, now 87 Lorna Road, was then named 'Savernake' – presumably by Jefferies himself – and was one of only eight newly-built houses on the street, overlooking railway tracks at the back, not far from Hove railway station.

Jefferies' observations of nature continued in Hove, with sunshine and willow wrens on the gorse, stonechats and meadow pipits, bats and weasels, and kestrels hovering around the very edge of the town. Curiously for a country lover, Jefferies chose Brighton & Hove (rather than places like Eastbourne) because of the lack of trees – it was a common belief that fewer trees led to a 'drier' atmosphere, which was better for recuperation from illnesses like his. Despite the desire for dry air however, the writer still enjoyed taking walks along the shore, and loved the sea.

One of the other benefits of Hove was its proximity to the Sussex Downs, where Jefferies also loved to roam. The green hills around Brighton reminded the author of the security blanket of the Wiltshire Downs of his earlier life which, as his writing shows, he was clearly missing.

ABOVE: Stone plaque on 87 Lorna Road, Hove, although the dates don't correspond with Jefferies' own notes about when he moved there. The house is just a few metres away from Selborne Place – a curious, and probably coincidental, link to that other famous nature writer, Gilbert White.

RIGHT: Grand Avenue in Hove, still dominated by Queen Victoria, as it was in Jefferies' day.

"Lands of gold have been found, and lands of spices and precious merchandise; but this is the land of health."

Nature Near London

165

Something Wanting

Many of Jefferies' articles and essays ended up as collections printed in book form. In February 1883, six months after arriving in Hove, such a collection, written originally for *The Standard*, was accepted for publication by *Chatto and Windus* under the title *Nature Near London.* Recounting the richness of nature in Surbiton and from observations in London itself, the book shows a more subtle, sensitive side to the author. The articles delve deeper into detail and demonstrate a perhaps more emotive response to the world, taking in less tangible aspects of nature, such as changes in colour or sound, and the feelings these things evoke. And there was something else: one of the benefits of turning the articles into a book was that it gave Jefferies an opportunity to write a retrospective introduction. In it he observes that for all the beauty and interest that London held there was nowhere "I could stretch myself in slumberous ease and watch the swallows ever wheeling, wheeling in the sky. This was the unseen influence of mighty London." Jefferies felt that something was wanting, and that something "was the absolute quiet, peace, and rest which dwells in the meadows and under the trees and on the hilltops in the country. Under its power the mind gradually yields itself to the green earth, the wind among the trees, the song of birds, and comes to have an understanding with them all." A letter from Jefferies to the publishing company *Longmans, Green, & Co.*, in June 1883, offers a new book in which the author attempts to describe how he yearned and struggled to attain such an understanding, while also openly condemning greed and injustice.

The book, which Jefferies said he had been meditating for seventeen years since his days on Liddington Hill back in Wiltshire, is called *The Story of My Heart* and subtitled *An Autobiography.* But this short book is not like any other autobiography. Firstly, it is not a chronological recounting of events, and secondly, most of the text is about life in general, not Jefferies specifically. The autobiography element was simply a practical way for Jefferies to alert potential publishers, and readers, that this was neither a work of fiction nor one of his more regular essays in nature or agriculture. Instead, *The Story of My Heart* is a book of inner thoughts and feelings; Jefferies called it "an actual record of thought." So although the title may seem misleading, it is hiding a real truth: the book is genuinely about Jefferies and his life, insofar as it is a result of his years observing and responding to the confusions, contradictions and complications of nature and of human kind.

One of the themes that runs through the whole book is that of time, or rather the absence of time. Jefferies describes a sort of mindfulness, or living in the moment, that emerged from his personal experiences in the endless cycles of nature: "I am in it now, not to-morrow, this moment; I cannot escape from it."

The book also explores broader ideas in time, such as human failures of the past and possibilities for the future.

Sadly for Jefferies, *The Story of My Heart* was not particularly well received in his own time, but it has been in print almost constantly since. Its contents really are a record of thought – the thoughts of one man's time on Earth, with all its flaws and faults, all its hopes and wishes, and its yearning for understanding, equality, peace and rest.

LEFT: Grandfather clock which has long since given up telling the time, at the Richard Jefferies Museum.

ABOVE: Plaque on Liddington Hill, used for target practice by troops stationed nearby in advance of D-Day 1945.

RIGHT: Liddington Hill, pastel drawing by Tara Parker-Woolway.

"It is eternity now. I am in the midst of it. It is about me in the sunshine; I am in it, as the butterfly floats in the light-laden air. Nothing has to come; it is now. Now is eternity; now is the immortal life. Here this moment, by this tumulus, on earth, now; I exist in it. The years, the centuries, the cycles are absolutely nothing; it is only a moment since this tumulus was raised; in a thousand years it will still be only a moment. To the soul there is no past and no future; all is and will be ever, in now. For artificial purposes time is mutually agreed on, but is really no such thing. The shadow goes on upon the dial, the index moves round upon the clock, and what is the difference? None whatever. If the clock had never been set going, what would have been the difference? There may be time for the clock, the clock may make time for itself; there is none for me.

I dip my hand in the brook and feel the stream; in an instant the particles of water which first touched me have floated yards down the current, my hand remains there. I take my hand away, and the flow – the time – of the brook does not exist to me. The great clock of the firmament, the sun and the stars, the crescent moon, the earth circling two thousand times, is no more to me than the flow of the brook when my hand is withdrawn; my soul has never been, and never can be, dipped in time. Time has never existed, and never will; it is a purely artificial arrangement. It is eternity now, it always was eternity, and always will be. By no possible means could I get into time if I tried. I am in eternity now and must there remain. Haste not, be at rest, this Now is eternity. Because the idea of time has left my mind – if ever it had any hold on it – to me the man interred in the tumulus is living now as I live. We are both in eternity."

The Story of My Heart

Divide and Share

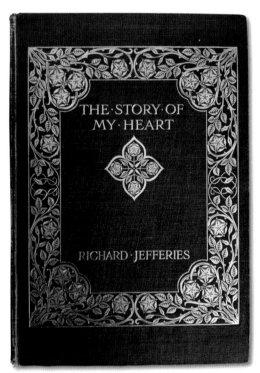

In terms of impetus for *The Story of My Heart*, it may have been that Jefferies' illness had alerted him to his own mortality and served as a catalyst to his new way of thinking; this new consciousness. Or it could have been the fact that his wife Jessie was expecting another child around this time, making him ponder the intrinsic value of human life. Or it may have been the realisation that, reliant as he was on sporadic payments from publishers, and with medical bills wiping out his savings, he himself was only one step away from that "abominable institution, the poorhouse." Jefferies also wrote several essays around the same period exploring the same ideas, including *Sun and Brook, On the Downs, Nature and Eternity,* and *The Dawn.* Although we know that it all began with a moment of inspiration back in Jefferies' late teens on a hill in Wiltshire, *The Story of My Heart* and the other essays of the time are the first pieces of his writing to really let such thoughts rise to the surface, marking a radical departure from everything else the author had done.

It is not easy to categorise such a book since it does not conform to any particular literary genre, just one man's thoughts with no other apparent common thread. But there are a number of broad themes, as well as the exploration of time. As would be expected of anything Jefferies wrote, the book revolves around nature and our relationship with it (and with each other), but in a much more ethereal, spiritual, and sometimes ruthless way than most of his previous work. As well as celebrating the marvels of the natural world with phrases such as "It is enough to lie on the sward in the shadow of green boughs, to listen to the songs of summer, to drink in the sunlight, the air, the flowers, the sky, the beauty of all," Jefferies also accepts that "The sea, the earth, the sun, the trees, the hills, care nothing for human life," and "The earth, though loved so dearly, would let me perish on the ground, and neither bring forth food nor water. Burning in the sky the great sun, of whose company I have been so fond, would merely burn on and make no motion to assist me."

There is also a hope, or wish, that we could change our position in the natural order: an idea that humans have the power to dictate how they exist, and even for how long, through the recognition and development of our own souls, without resigning ourselves to a fate governed by a greater intelligence. This thinly veiled rejection of many religious beliefs of the time is accompanied by a rejection of what Jefferies sees as other commonly held 'wisdoms' which govern the way humans live. In particular, the author's newly expressed antipathy towards the hardships of the farm labourers is explored, in broader terms, with very strongly worded condemnations of poverty and the 'interested ignorance' which

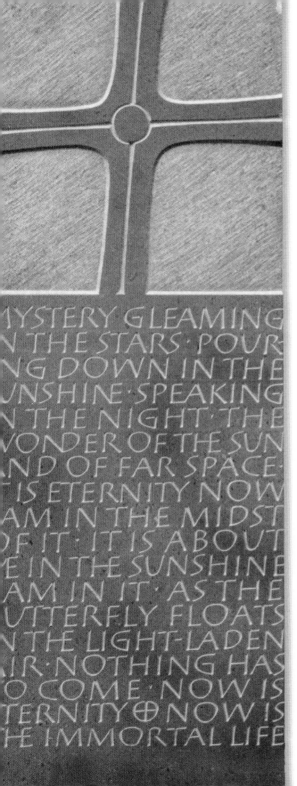

propagates the unfair work practices which cause it. In 1875, in *Restless Human Hearts,* Jefferies condemned millionaires for not sharing their 'superfluous gold', asking: "What on earth do they do with their money? They cannot eat it nor drink it all, nor spend it all on horse-racing and yachting." *The Story of My Heart* takes this idea further, suggesting that while the wealthiest people in Victorian society drive others to work for their gain, we would be better off devoting time to improving life for all through sharing the world's abundance. This would free us to embrace the idea that "Idleness – that is, the absence of the necessity to work for subsistence – is a great good. I hope succeeding generations will be able to be ideal. I hope that nine-tenths of their time will be leisure time; that they may enjoy their days, and the earth, and the beauty of this beautiful world; that they may rest by the sea and dream; that they may dance and sing, and eat and drink."

"I would submit to a severe discipline, and to go without many things cheerfully, for the good and happiness of the human race in the future. Each one of us should do something, however small, towards that great end."

The Story of My Heart

FAR LEFT: 1912 Duckworth & Co. edition of 'The Story of My Heart'.
LEFT: Words from the book carved in stone, by Tom Perkins.

"At this hour, out of thirty-four millions who inhabit this country, two-thirds – say twenty-two millions – live within thirty years of that abominable institution the poorhouse. That any human being should dare to apply to another the epithet "pauper" is, to me, the greatest, the vilest, the most unpardonable crime that could be committed. Each human being, by mere birth, has a birthright in this earth and all its productions; and if they do not receive it, then it is they who are injured, and it is not the "pauper" – oh, inexpressibly wicked word! – it is the well-to-do, who are the criminal classes.

It matters not in the least if the poor be improvident, or drunken, or evil in any way. Food and drink, roof and clothes, are the inalienable right of every child born into the light. If the world does not provide it freely – not as a grudging gift but as a right, as a son of the house sits down to breakfast – then is the world mad. But the world is not mad, only in ignorance – an interested ignorance, kept up by strenuous exertions, from which infernal darkness it will, in course of time, emerge, marvelling at the past as a man wonders at and glories in the light who has escaped from blindness."

The Story of My Heart

Victorian Poverty

Being poor in Victorian times was absolute: there was no welfare state and little charity; being poor could mean death. For those in rural areas, poverty was caused by the vagaries of the harvest – either by a failure of a poor farmer's own crops, or a meagre harvest reducing opportunities for seasonal harvest work. And of course other disruptions to normal life, such as war or politics, could also affect food prices and job opportunities. For example, the Irish Potato Famine of 1845-9 caused an estimated one million deaths and forced up to two million people to emigrate to England, Scotland and North America, often to more urban areas. But things weren't any better in the cities, with life for the poor still being a world away from that of the burgeoning middle classes. In the third verse of *All Things Bright and Beautiful*, published in 1848, Cecil Frances Alexander penned these lines: "The rich man in his castle, The poor man at his gate, God made them, high and lowly, And order'd their estate". This reflected the accepted view that there was a God-given hierarchy in society. In addition, there was the commonly held belief that the poor fell into two categories: with the 'deserving' poor, who were those considered unable to work because of reasons beyond their control (such as old age or infirmity), and the much larger number of 'undeserving' poor who were those who were believed to have caused their own destitution through things such as alcohol, fecklessness or prostitution.

As a result, there was growing concern in the early nineteenth century amongst the middle and upper classes that help being offered, through their taxes, was causing laziness and dependence amongst the poor. To shake up the system, the 1834 Poor Law Amendment Act reduced direct help and created a new welfare system based on the workhouse.

The first purpose-built workhouse was constructed in Abingdon, Oxfordshire in 1835; in total around 1800 were established. They were designed to maintain life, just, but deliberately offered a standard of living lower than that of a labourer outside. They became a shameful last resort for the poor. Families were separated upon entry, made to work for their upkeep, and had to wear a uniform. Conditions were intentionally monotonous and relentlessly physically exhausting. Many poor families spent their entire lifetimes in and out of the workhouse as their economic fortunes fluctuated. Aside from the workhouse, there were few options for the relief of poverty, and none of them lifted an individual out of poverty instead merely keeping them alive for the time being. Children in poor families were put to work as soon as they were able and although some charities did exist to assist the poor, support was piecemeal and often related to moral guidance rather than actual help. In reality, most of the poor were unable to make 'better' choices because of the shackles of poverty. It would not be until the end of the nineteenth century that social reformers began to argue in earnest that poverty was in fact the root of so many social problems, not the result of laziness or moral deficiency on the part of the poor.

"This is, indeed an extraordinary spectacle. That twelve thousand written years should have elapsed, and the human race – able to reason and to think, and easily capable of combination in immense armies for its own destruction – should still live from hand to mouth, like cattle and sheep, like the animals of the field and the birds of the woods; that there should not even be roofs to cover the children born, unless those children labour and expend their time to pay for them; that there should not be clothes, unless, again, time and labour are expended to procure them; that there should not be even food for the children of the human race, except they labour as their fathers did twelve thousand years ago; that even water should scarce be accessible to them, unless paid for by labour! In twelve thousand written years the world has not yet built itself a House, nor filled a Granary, nor organised itself for its own comfort. It is so marvellous I cannot express the wonder with which it fills me. And more wonderful still, if that could be, there are people so infatuated, or, rather, so limited of view, that they glory in this state of things, declaring that work is the main object of man's existence – work for subsistence – and glorying in their wasted time. To argue with such is impossible; to leave them is the only resource.

This our earth this day produces sufficient for our existence. This our earth produces not only a sufficiency, but a superabundance, and pours a cornucopia of good things down upon us. Further, it produces sufficient for stores and granaries to be filled to the rooftree for years ahead. I verily believe that the earth in one year produces enough food to last for thirty. Why, then, have we not enough? Why do people die of starvation, or lead a miserable existence on the verge of it? Why have millions upon millions to toil from morning to evening just to gain a mere crust of bread? Because of the absolute lack of organisation by which such labour should produce its effect, the absolute lack of distribution, the absolute lack even of the very idea that such things are possible. Nay, even to mention such things, to say that they are possible, is criminal with many. Madness could hardly go farther.

That selfishness has all to do with it I entirely deny. The human race for ages upon ages has been enslaved by ignorance and by interested persons whose object it has been to confine the minds of men, thereby doing more injury than if with infected hands they purposely imposed disease on the heads of the people. Almost worse than these, and at the present day as injurious, are those persons incessantly declaring, teaching, and impressing upon all that to work is man's highest condition. This falsehood is the interested superstition of an age infatuated with money, which having accumulated it cannot even expend it in pageantry. It is a falsehood propagated for the doubtful benefit of two or three out of ten thousand. It is the lie of a morality founded on money only, and utterly outside and having no association whatever with the human being in itself. Many superstitions have been got rid of in these days; time it is that this, the last and worst, were eradicated."

The Story of My Heart

177

Beautiful Human Life

As if to confirm Jefferies' idea that we should be making life better for future generations, July 18th 1883 saw a new addition to the family with the arrival of Richard Oliver Launcelot Jefferies, a younger brother for Harold and Phyllis, now eight and two-and-a-half years old respectively. Around this time, with the eye of a proud father, the author explored a belief that humans had the capacity to reach an ideal, both spiritually and "in the perfection of their physical frames," if they chose to work towards such an end. Of course, such thoughts also reflected the fact that Jefferies himself was far from such an ideal, with illness starting to take a real hold on his own body.

The search for a better environment for his health was to continue for the rest of Jefferies' life, next moving his newly enlarged family, in 1884, to take up residence in Eltham in Kent. But moving home and having another child did not slow down the writing, even to the point that the publishers *Longmans, Green, & Co.* warned him he was writing too much. Jefferies answered: "You tell me I write too much. To me it seems as if I write nothing, more especially since my illness." Unsurprisingly, much of the outpouring of work was in the form of essays about nature, such as the collection published as *The Life of the Fields*. Even then, the anger about poverty and politics was still there; for example, in one of the essays he penned around this time, *One of the New Voters,* Jefferies registers his disgust at farm workers being treated as animals.

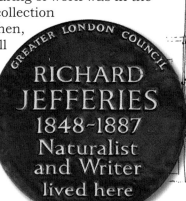

GREATER LONDON COUNCIL

RICHARD JEFFERIES 1848~1887 Naturalist and Writer lived here

His next publication, however, was a novel, *The Dewy Morn*. Essentially, the book is a love story, and was described by leading critic of the time, Q. D. Leavis,

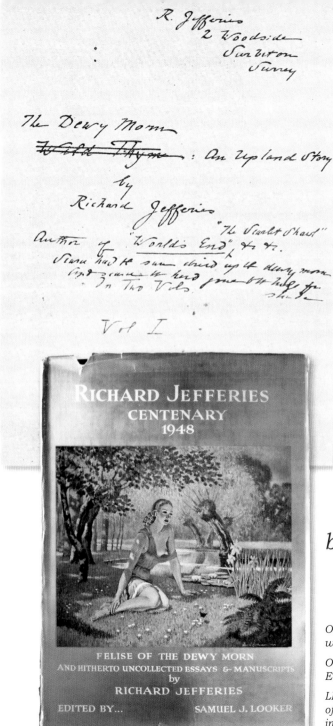

as "one of the few real novels between *Wuthering Heights* and *Sons and Lovers*," in which Jefferies "goes further than any Victorian novelist towards the modern novel." The book continues the author's railing against injustice, with depictions of tragedy among farm workers, and satirical digs at the upper classes. The most striking element of the book however, is the central character and heroine, Felise Goring. Felise is Jefferies' characterisation of love, in all its variants, and she is described as the perfect being which he wishes we would all aspire to.

Jefferies wrote about the perfect form elsewhere around this time: in *Nature in the Louvre*, he describes a statue he had seen in Paris, the *Vénus Accroupie*. Just as some aspects of Felise's description could be seen to verge on the erotic, so the description of the naked female torso was deemed improper by *Longmans, Green, & Co.*, who, at the time, refused to publish it.

> ## "O beautiful human life! Tears come in my eyes as I think of it. So beautiful, so inexpressibly beautiful!"
>
> *The Story of My Heart*

OPPOSITE TOP: Harold 'Toby' Jefferies, and Jessie 'Phyllis' Jefferies with her grandfather, James Jefferies.

OPPOSITE BOTTOM: 14 Victoria Road (now 59 Footscray Road), Eltham, Kent, and its blue plaque.

LEFT: Cover sheet for original manuscript of 'The Dewy Morn', and cover of a 1948 book published to celebrate the centenary of Jefferies' birth, including a risqué illustration of Felise, of 'The Dewy Morn'.

"The lane became more rugged; then there was a sudden dip, and in the hollow of the dip a streamlet ran across. A blackbird had been splashing in the water; and, as she came over the slope, rose up loudly calling. He perched on the hedge, looked towards her impudently from his dark eyes, half a mind to defy her, so bold was he in his beauty of blackest black and tawny bill. But as she stepped nearer he went off, again loudly calling and startling every bird in the field. The streamlet was so shallow the small flints were only half submerged, and the water was but a few inches wide. The sand which the blackbird had disturbed floated quickly away, leaving it perfectly pure. Felise stooped, dipped her fingers, and watched the drops fall sparkling from them. She felt the water, she liked to touch all things – the sunlight shone the brighter on her hand because it was wet.

Beyond the streamlet the lane rose rapidly, rugged and narrow; the hedges ceased, and only a hawthorn-bush here and there appeared on the banks. Presently it became a deep white groove, worn in chalk. Felise stepped quickly now, and in a few minutes reached the foot of the hill, where the lane left the straight line, and went up the Downs aslant, so that waggons might be drawn up, which they could not have been had the track been straight.

The moment Felise's foot touched the sward, she began to run up the hill, making direct for the ridge like a hare, or a bee bent for the thyme above. Her arched insteps, like springs, threw her forwards; her sinews, strung and strong, lifted her easily. Her weight did not press the turf—it was for the time suspended between her swift bounds. Rejoicing, her deep chest opened, the pliant ribs, like opening fingers, made room for cubic feet of purest atmosphere. The air inhaled lifted her; she was lighter and more swift.

Forced into the blood, the strong hill air intoxicated her. She forgot all; she saw nothing – neither the sun, the sky, nor the slope itself; her entire being was occupied in putting forth her strength. Up – from thyme-bunch to thyme-bunch; past gray flat flints; past rusty ironstone fragments; past the parallel paths, a few inches wide, which streaked the hill – up, straight for the summit!

A lark, startled, fled, but immediately began to soar and sing. The landscape widened beneath; there were woods and bright fields. She did not see the fields, or woods, or hear the lark; nor notice the flints which, like lesser mile-stones, marked her run. Her limbs grew stronger, her bounds more powerful, as her breath was drawn in long, deep inspirations. The labour increased her strength; her appetite for the work grew as she went. She ran and drank the wind to have more of herself – to have the fulness of her own existence, the great heart within her throbbed and bore her, replying to her spirit.

More flints, more thyme – a stone-chat flitted away – longer grass, more slippery, the slope steeper, still – up! Yet the strong limbs could not bound quite so far; the feet fell as swiftly, but the space covered was not so wide. There was effort now.

Brave as may be the heart of woman, yet the high hills must try it. So great was the rush of the aërated blood, it seemed to threaten to suffocate her. The supple knees could not straighten themselves; they remained slightly bent. The pliant ribs, opened to their widest, seemed forced outwards by an expansive power which must break them to get free. Her head was thrown back: she did not look now at the ridge; she looked up at the sky. Surely the summit must be near?

She would have dropped rather than give up; she would have dropped like a hunted animal before she would have yielded.

The time when she knew she must fall was numbered now but by seconds. The strong air which at first gave such a sense of vigour was now too strong; it began to take away her breath. She did not feel her limbs; they moved mechanically, though still quickly. She saw nothing but the sky. Five seconds more, and down she must go: not even that great heart could bear more.

But she was nearer than she knew. Suddenly the slope became less steep, where the summit seemed planed away; her feet went along instead of having to be lifted. She looked and saw the thorn-bush on the ridge before her. She stopped by the bush; she had done it – the hill was conquered."

The Dewy Morn

"Turning to the left on entering the Louvre, I found myself at once among the sculpture, which is on the ground-floor. Except that the Venus of Milo was in the collection, I had no knowledge of what I was about to see, but stepped into an unknown world of statuary. Somewhat indifferently I glanced up and then down, and instantly my coolness was succeeded by delight, for there, in the centre of the gallery, was a statue in the sense in which I understand the word – the beautiful made tangible in human form. I said at once, That is my statue. There lies all Paris for me; I shall find nothing further. I was then at least thirty yards distant, with the view partly broken, but it was impossible to doubt or question lines such as those. On a gradual approach the limbs become more defined, and the torso grows, and becomes more and more human – this is one of the remarkable circumstances connected with the statue. There is life in the wide hips, chest, and shoulders; so marvellous is the illusion that not only the parts that remain appear animated, but the imagination restores the missing and mutilated pieces, and the statue seems entire. I did not see that the hand was missing and the arms gone; the idea of form suggested by the existing portions was carried on over these, and filled the vacant places.

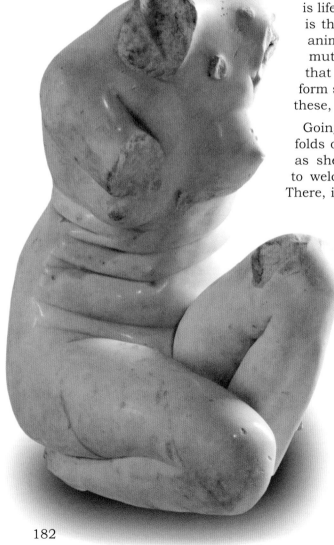

Going nearer, the large hips grow from stone to life, the deep folds of the lower torso have but this moment been formed as she stooped, and the impulse is to extend the hands to welcome this beautiful embodiment of loving kindness. There, in full existence, visible, tangible, seems to be all that the heart has imagined of the deepest and highest emotions. She stoops to please the children, that they may climb her back; the whole of her body speaks the dearest, the purest love. To extend the hands towards her is so natural, it is difficult to avoid actually doing so. Hers is not the polished beauty of the Venus de Medici, whose very fingers have no joints. The typical Venus is fined down from the full growth of human shape to fit the artist's conception of what beauty should be. Her frame is rounded; her limbs are rounded; her neck is rounded; the least possible appearance of fulness is removed; any line that is not in exact accordance with a strict canon is worked out – in short, an ideal

LEFT: the statue Jefferies describes above: the Vénus Accroupie - a 2nd-century crouching Venus from the collection of Louis XIV, in the Musée du Louvre.

RIGHT: the modern entrance to the Musée du Louvre, Paris.

is produced, but humanity is obliterated. Something of the too rounded is found in it – a figure so polished has an air of the bath and of the mirror, of luxury; it is too feminine; it obviously has a price payable in gold. But here is a woman perfect as a woman, with the love of children in her breast, her back bent for their delight. An ideal indeed, but real and human. Her form has its full growth of wide hips, deep torso, broad shoulders. Nothing has been repressed or fined down to a canon of art or luxury. A heart beats within her bosom; she is love; with her neither gold nor applause has anything to do; she thinks of the children. In that length of back and width of chest, in that strong torso, there is just the least trace of manliness. She is not all, not too feminine; with all her tenderness, she can think and act as nobly as a man."

Nature in the Louvre

No Greater Cruelty

A new toddler crawling around the new home, and the successful publication of *The Dewy Morn* and *The Life of the Fields* should have heralded a time of joy and prosperity for Jefferies, Jessie and the other two children. Tragically, this was not to be.

During 1884, Jefferies describes his symptoms as coughing, stomach problems and, consequently, poor sleep. By October the doctors had all but exhausted their knowledge in trying to identify the root of his problems, and the bills had all but exhausted the family's savings. A few months later, on 16th March 1885, fate played a worse hand, as young Richard Oliver Launcelot was struck down by an epidemic of meningitis and died aged only eighteen months. The shock to the family was clearly horrific, but somehow it struck Jefferies himself even harder, reminiscent of when he was a toddler and the death of his sister Ellen knocked everything out of his mother. Jefferies was so badly affected that he could not even bring himself to attend his young son's funeral. Decades later, in 1944, Launcelot's elder brother, Harold, recalled the time saying "the agonised expression on my father's face as he stood at the open door watching the little cortege slowly move away, haunted my mind for many years."

In Jefferies' own words: "nature gave way, and I broke down utterly."

Sickness and grief put the author onto his bed "half delirious and in the most dreadful state." A specialist, Dr Kidd, was requested to come down from London. The doctor diagnosed ulceration of the intestines and prescribed a diet of milk, malted food and shredded meat. Although Jefferies began to feel better after a couple of days, the decline in his health was far from halted and another house move was called for – Dr Kidd suggested that Jefferies should move to Tunbridge Wells, which had a reputation as a healthier place to live. The family stayed briefly in Rotherfield, before taking up residence at 'The Downs', on London Road, Crowborough, about ten miles from Tunbridge Wells. But neither the sickness nor this further house move stopped the work coming out, with the publication in early April of another novel, *After London*.

After London is set in England after some undescribed catastrophe has destroyed much of civilisation, and hugely reduced the population. Despite having been written earlier, Jefferies' bleak vision of a broken world, and an individual struggling against the odds, seems strangely apt for the dark period that he found himself in at the time of publication.

"Everything fell quickly into barbarism"

After London

RIGHT: Stone lintel above the door of 'The Downs' in Crowborough.
OPPOSITE: 'Dead London', by Henrique Alvim Corrêa.

This Great Catastrophe

After London is set in the distant future, when a historic catastrophe has turned the country 'wild' again, causing flooding, destruction, starvation and death across the land. In keeping with Jefferies' views of the ruling elite, "the richer and upper classes made use of their money to escape", never to be heard of again, leaving behind the most ignorant, those in remote areas, and poor farming communities.

On the face of it, *After London* appears to be a very different genre from everything Jefferies had written before. However, the title of a German version of the book translates as *The Forest Returns*, and instantly brings us back to familiar territory: the book describes a world where nature rules; plant and animal life everywhere; rewilding. Then, after the country "became green everywhere in the first spring, after London ended," the story becomes an odyssey of one man's struggle against the world and the evils of the people left behind. Admired by William Morris, and predating books like those of H. G. Wells by a decade, Jefferies had created the very first story of its kind, a new genre: post-apocalyptic fiction focused on the trials and triumphs of those who survive in an imagined future world.

OPPOSITE: Stained glass window depicting 'After London'.

ABOVE: 'After London' has been republished countless times, and in many languages.

Perhaps the most startling part of the book is the depiction of London itself, as a toxic, deadly swamp. Such a grim vision was typically Victorian, with the 'hero', Felix Aquila, taking on trials in a quest for love and higher ideals. Felix sets off in a canoe to explore the flood waters in a romanticised version of the world reminiscent of Jefferies' childhood on Coate Water, as recounted in *Bevis*. But it is Jefferies' understanding of nature and the raw countryside that gives the book its identity. Although the tale's causal disaster is not expressed, it is clearly an environmental issue, with tides rising and falling, oceans silting up, and greenery flourishing.

The notion of London melting into a swamp is the author's way of expressing a fear for the future of civilization. Jefferies knows that nature does not hold any special care for humankind, and describes nature's power to swiftly eradicate what he sees as the negative products of human activity. In Jefferies' nature-loving eye, this is a good thing, but also a warning. Although terms like environmental catastrophe, or natural disaster, or climate change are now commonplace, Jefferies knew that nature itself, though altered by events, will simply carry on. The disaster is, as he feared, for civilization. For the human race.

"The old men say their fathers told them that soon after the fields were left to themselves a change began to be visible. It became green everywhere in the first spring, after London ended, so that all the country looked alike.

The meadows were green, and so was the rising wheat which had been sown, but which neither had nor would receive any further care. Such arable fields as had not been sown, but where the last stubble had been ploughed up, were overrun with couch-grass, and where the short stubble had not been ploughed, the weeds hid it. So that there was no place which was not more or less green; the footpaths were the greenest of all, for such is the nature of grass where it has once been trodden on, and by-and-by, as the summer came on, the former roads were thinly covered with the grass that had spread out from the margin.

In the autumn, as the meadows were not mown, the grass withered as it stood, falling this way and that, as the wind had blown it; the seeds dropped, and the bennets became a greyish-white, or, where the docks and sorrel were thick, a brownish-red. The wheat, after it had ripened, there being no one to reap it, also remained standing, and was eaten by clouds of sparrows, rooks, and pigeons, which flocked to it and were undisturbed, feasting at their pleasure. As the winter came on, the crops were beaten down by the storms, soaked with rain, and trodden upon by herds of animals."

After London

LEFT: The 'rewilded' Knepp Estate, Sussex.

"Thus the low-lying parts of the mighty city of London became swamps, and the higher grounds were clad with bushes. The very largest of the buildings fell in, and there was nothing visible but trees and hawthorns on the upper lands, and willows, flags, reeds, and rushes on the lower. These crumbling ruins still more choked the stream, and almost, if not quite, turned it back. If any water ooze past, it is not perceptible, and there is no channel through to the salt ocean. It is a vast stagnant swamp, which no man dare enter, since death would be his inevitable fate.

There exhales from this oozy mass so fatal a vapour that no animal can endure it. The black water bears a greenish-brown floating scum, which for ever bubbles up from the putrid mud of the bottom. When the wind collects the miasma, and, as it were, presses it together, it becomes visible as a low cloud which hangs over the place. The cloud does not advance beyond the limit of the marsh, seeming to stay there by some constant attraction; and well it is for us that it does not, since at such times when the vapour is thickest, the very wildfowl leave the reeds, and fly from the poison. There are no fishes, neither can eels exist in the mud, nor even newts. It is dead.

The flags and reeds are coated with slime and noisome to the touch; there is one place where even these do not grow, and where there is nothing but an oily liquid, green and rank. It is plain there are no fishes in the water, for herons do not go thither, nor the kingfishers, not one of which approaches the spot. They say the sun is sometimes hidden by the vapour when it is thickest, but I do not see how any can tell this, since they could not enter the cloud, as to breathe it when collected by the wind is immediately fatal. For all the rottenness of a thousand years and of many hundred millions of human beings is there festering under the stagnant water, which has sunk down into and penetrated the earth, and floated up to the surface the contents of the buried cloacæ."

After London

191

Weary of Illness

Neither Jefferies nor his doctors knew it, but the illness that was taking hold of him was a rare form of tuberculosis which would only give him a couple more years to live. In September 1885 the author noted "my spine seemed suddenly to snap", leaving him practically paralysed on the sofa and confined to the house for seven months. During this time he was inevitably upset at being cut off from the outdoors he loved, and cursed his inability to write: "Often I am compelled to sit or lie for days and think, think, till I feel as if I should become insane, for my mind seems as clear as ever, and the anxiety and eager desire to do something is as strong as in my best days."

The thinking led to more ideas, either from memory or from jottings in his notebooks, and to more publications. Towards the end of the year a new series of essays was published as *The Open Air*. By now Jefferies had settled into a strong, rhythmic style of his own when it came to nature observations, and *The Open Air* is full of such characteristic work, full of passion for wildlife and making no apologies for simply stated opinions about human life: "The wheat is beautiful, but human life is labour."

Throughout 1886, Jefferies continued to work but was increasingly able to write only with the help of his wife, Jessie. This of course was on top of everything else Jessie had to do, with two children and

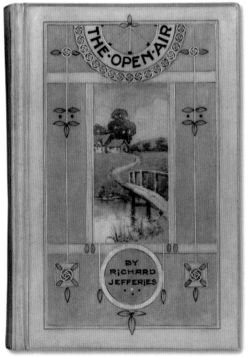

a household to look after. In a letter to his mother, Jefferies explains that Jessie hasn't had time to write personally since, "she has so much to do waiting on me all day for I cannot do the smallest thing for myself." And with little income plus medical bills, the family was sinking into ever deeper financial trouble; so much so that the publisher C. J. Longman suggested Jefferies should apply to the Royal Literary Fund for a charitable handout, even if just to pay for a holiday. The idea appalled Jefferies, who considered such charity to be more humiliating than being sent to the workhouse. However, in the end he did make an application and was awarded £50 from the fund. In the meantime, Longman organised a collection among Jefferies' supporters, and raised enough money to help the family move house again, this time to Goring-by-Sea.

Despite having moved away from the sea at Hove and to the high elevation of Crowborough for health reasons, the medical advice was now to be by the sea again. So, in October 1886, the family moved into *Seaview*. The house is now called *Jefferies House*, and the small cul-de-sac where it is situated has been renamed *Jefferies Lane*. It was to be the last house where Jefferies lived.

JEFFERIES
HOUSE

ABOVE: 'Seaview',
in Goring-by-Sea.

LEFT: The coast at
Goring-by-Sea.

OPPOSITE: Cover
of a later edition of
'The Open Air'.

193

Victorian Tuberculosis

Tubercolosis (TB) is a bacterial infection which usually affects the lungs of the patient, although it can affect other parts of the body, such as glands in the abdomen, bones, and/or the nervous system. It is not a new disease (evidence of tuberculosis has been found in Egyptian mummies), but widespread industrialisation in Victorian England and the rapid growth of overcrowded and insanitary towns and cities meant that incidences of tuberculosis reached their peak in the nineteenth century. Poor workers lived in cramped and damp conditions where it was easy for infection to spread. In 1815, 25% of all deaths were from tuberculosis in Britain, and half of patients who contracted the disease and were not treated died from it. Richard Jefferies was not the only individual in the world of the arts to succumb to the disease. Many more, including D.H. Lawrence, Emily Brontë, Frédéric Chopin and George Orwell, also died of tuberculosis.

Tuberculosis has historically been called a number of other names, including 'Captain of all these Men of Death', the 'White Plague' (a reference to the pallid complexion and wasting away of sufferers) and the 'Consumption'. 'Consumption' was a term of ancient Greek origin and was the name of the disease most commonly used in the nineteenth century, even after Johann Johann Schönlein named it tuberculosis in 1834. People knew that it was contagious, principally through coughing and sneezing, and were all too aware that once one person in a household was infected, it was highly likely that others would also become ill too. For this reason, tuberculosis was also referred to as the 'family attendant'. However, there was little understanding of the scientific causes of the disease. It was not until 1882 that the German scientist Robert Koch announced his discovery of the germ which caused tuberculosis. In 1895, Konrad Röntgen discovered x-rays which at last enabled doctors to see the effect of tuberculosis on the lungs and other organs in a non-invasive way, and this aided diagnosis of the condition. However, it was the 1940s and 1950s before the first effective treatments for TB were found.

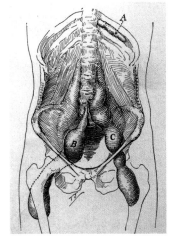

In the nineteeth century, in the absence of any effective pharmaceutical intervention, treatment centred around the provision of clean air to clear the lungs, a balanced diet, and isolation to prevent the spread of infection. This threefold technique was pioneered by Hermann Brehmer in Germany in 1854. In 1868 The Royal National Hospital for Chest Diseases was built on the Isle of Wight where its founder, Arthur Hill Hassell, shared Brehmer views. Patients were housed in single rooms, were well fed and exposed to clean and natural air, rest and quiet. Many other hospitals, known as sanatoriums, were built in the UK to treat patients for long term illness, principally tuberculosis. Patients could stay there for months, if not years.

"The front of the British Museum stands in the sunlight clearly marked against the firm blue of the northern sky. The blue appears firm as if solid above the angle of the stonework, for while looking towards it – towards the north – the rays do not come through the azure, which is therefore colour without life. It seems nearer than the southern sky, it descends and forms a close background to the building; as you approach you seem to come nearer to the blue surface rising at its rear.

The dark edges of sloping stone are distinct and separate, but not sharp; the hue of the stone is toned by time and weather, and is so indefinite as to have lost its hardness. Those small rounded bodies upon the cornice are pigeons resting in the sun, so motionless and neutral-tinted that they might be mistaken for some portion of the carving. A double gilt ring, a circle in a circle, at the feet of an allegorical figure gleams brightly against the dark surface.

The sky already seems farther away seen between the boles of stone, perpetual shade dwells in their depth, but two or three of the pigeons fluttering down are searching for food on the sunlit gravel at the bottom of the steps. To them the building is merely a rock, pierced with convenient caverns; they use its exterior for their purpose, but penetrate no farther.

With air and light, the sunlit gravel, the green lawn between it and the outer railings – with these they are concerned, and with these only. The heavy roll of the traffic in Oxford Street, audible here, is nothing to them; the struggle for money does not touch them, they let it go by. Nor the many minds searching and re-searching in the great Library, this mental toil is no more to them than the lading of the waggons in the street.

Neither the tangible product nor the intellectual attainment is of any value – only the air and light."

The Pigeons at the British Museum, The Open Air

197

The Sun Declines

Eventually Jefferies had to abandon his writing desk altogether, with his very last essay *My Old Village* being dictated to Jessie. But before he reached that stage, the author managed to write one final book: a novel titled *Amaryllis at the Fair,* set around the life of a young lady at the time of the May Fair. The book is essentially autobiographical, with Amaryllis living in a representation of Coate Farm with her parents, Iden and Mrs Iden, who are clearly Jefferies' own father and mother. The book initially met with some opposition from publishers and even after its publication by *Sampson Low,* in March 1887, it continued to divide opinion, mainly over whether or not it was a novel at all. It is true that the book does not conform to any model of fiction. It starts like a classic novel of the time, with Amaryllis describing the men she sees over the garden wall, on their way to the fair, and weighing up their good and not so good points. But as the book unfurls Jefferies lets his own thoughts come to the fore: his family, political views, comments about seemingly random subjects, and life in general. Despite this, or because of it, the book attracted praise from some highly respected literary critics: Q. D. Leavis called the book 'a masterpiece,' while Edward Garnet said he would turn out several highly-regarded Thomas Hardy novels to make room on his shelf for it.

As a biographical piece *Amaryllis at the Fair* takes Jefferies back to his home at Coate again, with vivid characterisations of his parents (especially his father), complete with criticisms but clearly full of love and affection. In particular the author yearns for the couple's happiness, wishing for a timepiece for mother, and nice food like fish and wine, and for the debtors to back off and give father just one day's peace. Nature is there of course, and politics too, both family and national, with "revolutionary Amaryllis, the red-hot republican blood seething like molten metal in her veins." As the plot drifts, guests Amadis and

Alere arrive and the book becomes increasingly philosophical, with debates in the tranquil setting of the summer house "properly builded of brick, as a summer-house should be."

The way the conversation flows, and moves around, feels like a joining up of a circle, with the author looking back over his life. The conflicting sides of Jefferies shine through the characters: the talented genius, shaking from years of drudgery at work, and the poor, sick, unsure intellect. And, above all, the young, vibrant, healthy artist who is so in awe of the beauty and power of nature that there lingers not the slightest ambition to ever capture it through art; who stands up to greed and injustice; who would do anything to have happy parents; and has been lucky enough to know love.

RIGHT: *Drawing of the summer house at Coate Farm, by H.E. Tidmarsh, from the 1946 'Worthing Cavalcade – Richard Jefferies: A Tribute.'*

LEFT: *Oil painting, by Jane Milner-Barry, of Jefferies' attic bedroom at Coate Farm, as described in 'Amaryllis at the Fair': "her study, her thinking-room, her private chapel and praying-room, her one place of solitude, silence, and retirement."*

"Here was Amaryllis, very strong and full of life, very, very young and inexperienced, very poor and without the least expectation whatever (for who could reconcile the old and the older Iden?), the daughter of poor and embarrassed parents, whom she wished and prayed to help in their coming old age. Here was Amaryllis, full of poetic feeling and half a painter at heart, full of generous sentiments – what a nature to be ground down in the sordidness of married poverty!

Here was Amadis, extremely poor, quite feeble, and unable to earn a shilling, just talking of seeing the doctor again about this fearful debility, full too, as he thought at least, of ideas – what a being to think of her!

Nothing ever happens in the fitness of things. If only now he could have regained the health and strength of six short months ago – if only that, but you see, he had not even that. He might get better; true, he might, I have tried 80 drugs and I am no better, I hope he will.

There they sat, happier and happier, and deeper and deeper in love every moment, on the brown timber in the long grass, their hearts as full of love as the meadow was of sunshine.

You have heard of the Sun's Golden Cup, in which after sunset he was carried over Ocean's stream, while we slumber in the night, to land again in the East and give us the joy of his rising. The great Golden Cup in which Hercules, too, was taken over; it was as if that Cup had been filled to the brim with the nectar of love and placed at the lips to drink, inexhaustible.

I shall leave Amaryllis and Amadis in their Interlude in Heaven. Let the Play of Human Life, with its sorrows and its Dread, pause awhile; let Care go aside behind the wings, let Debt and Poverty unrobe, let Age stand upright, let Time stop still (oh, Miracle! as the Sun did in the Vale of Ajalon). Let us leave our lovers in the Interlude in Heaven.

And as I must leave them (I trust but for a little while) I will leave them on the brown oak timber, sap-stain brown, in the sunshine and dancing shadow of summer, among the long grass and the wild flowers."

Amaryllis at the Fair

LEFT: the grasses and wild flowers at Jefferies' birthplace, under the sunshine and the shadow of the holm oak

What is life?

Edward William Garnett (1868–1937) was an English writer, critic and literary editor. He played an instrumental part in getting D. H. Lawrence's *Sons and Lovers* published, and in an essay about *Amaryllis at the Fair*, he captures not only the value of this one book, but of Jefferies' singular skill in capturing the essence of nature and agriculture, our relationship with them, and with each other:

"How true, how unerringly true to human nature is this picture of the Iden household; how delicately felt and rendered to a hair is his picture of the father's sluggish, masculine will, pricked ineffectually by the waspish tongue of feminine criticism. Further, we not only have the family's idiosyncrasies, their habits, mental atmosphere, and domestic story brought before us in a hundred pages, easily and instinctively by the hand of the artist, but we have the whole book steeped in the breath of English spring, the restless ache of spring that thrills through the nerves, and stirs the sluggish winter blood; we have the spring feeling breaking from the March heavens and the March earth in copse, meadow, and ploughland, as it has scarcely been rendered before by English novelist.

"The book shows the carelessness, the haste, the roughness of a sketch, a sketch, moreover, which Jefferies was not destined to carry to the end he had planned, but we repeat, let us be thankful that its artistic weaknesses are those of a sketch direct from nature, rather than those of an ambitious studio picture. And these digressions are an integral part of the book's character, just as the face of a man has its own blemishes: they are one with the spirit of the whole, and so, if they break somewhat the illusion of the scenes, they do not damage its spiritual unity. It is this spiritual unity on which we must insist, because *Amaryllis* is indeed Jefferies' last and complete testament on human life. He wrote it, or rather dictated it to his wife, as he lay in pain, slowly dying, and he has put into it the frankness of a dying man. How real, how solid, how deliciously sweet seemed those simple earthly joys, those human appetites of healthy, vigorous men to him! how intense is his passion and spiritual hunger for the beauty of earth! Like a flame shooting up from the log it is consuming, so this passion for the green earth, for the earth in wind and rain and sunshine, consumes the wasted, consumptive body of the dying man. The reality, the solidity of the homely farmhouse life he describes spring from the intensity with which he clings to all he loves, the cold March wind buffeting the face, the mating cries of the birds in the hot spring sunshine. Life is so terribly strong, so deliciously real, so full of man's unsatisfied hungry ache for happiness; and sweet is the craving, bitter the knowledge of the unfulfilment. So, inspiring and vivifying the whole, in every line of *Amaryllis* is Jefferies' philosophy of life. Jefferies 'did not understand human nature,' say the accomplished critics. Did he not? *Amaryllis at the Fair* is one of the truest criticisms of human life, oh reader, you are likely to meet with. The mixedness of things, the old, old human muddle, the meanness and stupidity and shortsightedness of humanity, the good salty taste of life in the healthy mouth, the spirituality of love, the strong earthy roots of appetite, man's lust of life, with circumstances awry, and the sharp wind blowing alike on the just and the unjust – all is there on the printed page of *Amaryllis at the Fair*."

"How can you draw life itself? What is life? you cannot even define it. The swallow's wing has the motion of life – its tremble – its wonderful delicacy of vibration – the instant change – the slip of the air; – no man will ever be able to draw a flying swallow."

Amaryllis at the Fair

LEFT: Adaptation of one of the covers of 'Amaryllis at the Fair' – a laser-cut steel depiction of Amaryllis looking over the wall at the revellers on their way to the fair.

"No one else seems to have seen the sparkle on the brook, or heard the music at the hatch, or to have felt back through the centuries; and when I try to describe these things to them they look at me with stolid incredulity. No one seems to understand how I got food from the clouds, nor what there was in the night, nor why it is not so good to look at it out of window. They turn their faces away from me, so that perhaps after all I was mistaken, and there never was any such place or any such meadows, and I was never there. And perhaps in course of time I shall find out also, when I pass away physically, that as a matter of fact there never was any earth."

My Old Village - Jefferies' last essay.

Calmly to Death

Jefferies' final writings were edited by Jessie after her husband's death and published later, in 1889, as *Field and Hedgerow*. In their respective biographies of Jefferies, Andrew Rossabi describes the last essays as "Some of Jefferies' finest and most moving papers," and Edward Thomas says, "both in their mingling of reflection and description, and in their abundant play of emotion, they stand by themselves and enlarge the boundaries of this typical form of English prose." Jefferies was still writing, about his beloved wild life, right up to the end of his life.

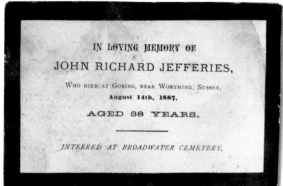

On 14th August 1887 Jefferies died, aged just 38. The tuberculosis which had affected his lungs and bowels, and probably his spine too, finally defeated him. In his own words "death triumphed." He had declared that, if he could, he would have his body burned on a pine-wood funeral pyre, on top of a hill in the open air, his ashes "freely sown wide and broadcast." Sadly this was not an option and Jefferies was buried in nearby Broadwater & Worthing Cemetery.

Despite having often declared opposition to organised religion the author was given a Christian burial and his grave was marked by a stone cross. As well as predeceasing his parents, two brothers and sister, he left behind Jessie and their two remaining children, Harold (aged 12) and Phyllis (aged 6½).

"So trustful are the doves, the squirrels, the birds of the branches, and the creatures of the field. Under their tuition let us rid ourselves of mental terrors, and face death itself as calmly as they do the livid lightning; so trustful and so content with their fate, resting in themselves and unappalled."

The Pageant of Summer

IN
EVER LOVING MEMORY
OF

JOHN RICHARD JEFFERIES
WHO DIED AT GORING
AUGUST 14th 1887, AGED 38 YEARS

ALSO IN MEMORY OF RICHARD OLIVER LAUNCELOT
HIS BELOVED YOUNGEST CHILD
WHO DIED MARCH 16th ... AGED ... MONTHS

...ry of the Prose Poet of Englands fields and woodlan...

ABOVE & LEFT: Richard Jefferies' grave in Broadwater & Worthing Cemetery, as it was and as it is now.

OPPOSITE: Jefferies' death card.

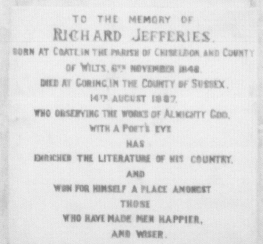

TO THE MEMORY OF

RICHARD JEFFERIES.

BORN AT COATE, IN THE PARISH OF CHISELDON AND COUNTY
OF WILTS, 6TH NOVEMBER 1848.
DIED AT GORING, IN THE COUNTY OF SUSSEX.
14TH AUGUST 1887.
WHO OBSERVING THE WORKS OF ALMIGHTY GOD,
WITH A POET'S EYE
HAS
ENRICHED THE LITERATURE OF HIS COUNTRY,
AND
WON FOR HIMSELF A PLACE AMONGST
THOSE
WHO HAVE MADE MEN HAPPIER,
AND WISER.

BACKGROUND: Marble bust of Jefferies in Salisbury Cathedral, created in 1891 by Margaret Thomas.

208

Legacy

Noted for Generations

As so often seems to happen to notable people, Jefferies' star really rose after his death. In the immediate aftermath, at the end of the nineteenth century, books that were worth a few shillings suddenly became worth guineas and the printing of new editions began – including the *Pocket Richard Jefferies*, a copy of which is known to have been bought by Thomas Hardy, the most famous writer about rural life in the 1800s. For seventy five years or more Richard Jefferies was a household name, with children being given *Bevis* and *Wood Magic* for their birthday; graduates learning about him at university; schools, streets and buildings named in his honour; Prime Ministers and celebrities mentioning him; plaques everywhere; and even mentions in popular literature. In 1910, E. M. Forster's *Howard's End* was published. In it was the following line: "Curious it should all come about from reading something of Richard Jefferies."

In the early twentieth century, artists like Kate Tryon (see pages 108 & 142) were inspired by Jefferies, and, as the world headed towards the Great War of 1914-18, the author found a new raft of literary supporters, including Henry Williamson, Charles Sorley and Edward Thomas, all who went on to serve in the war. Influenced enormously by Jefferies, Williamson later became a leading nature writer himself, with his classics like *Tarka the Otter*; in 1913, before gaining renown as a war poet, Sorley penned a poem about Jefferies, "the man from Coate;" and Thomas, who was feasibly England's greatest nature poet as well as one of the great war poets before his death in 1917, wrote about Jefferies' life and works in what has been described as "one of the finest literary biographies in the language."

In 1932, E. H. Shepard, the world famous illustrator of A. A. Milne's *Winnie-the-Pooh*, provided drawings for *Bevis*. Milne's son, 'Christopher Robin' Milne later selected *Bevis* as his Desert Island book on the Radio Four programme, calling it the book that inspired his childhood. He added that he had read *Bevis* more often than any other book, and even carried it with him throughout his army service in World War II. And *Bevis* has other connections to well-known literature; for example, Arthur Ransome loved the book as a child, long before he went on to write *Swallows and Amazons*; and John Fowles, in the 1976 foreword to his classic *The Magus*, says, "The second influence may seem surprising, but it was undoubtedly that of a book which haunted my childhood imagination, Richard Jefferies' *Bevis*. I believe novelists are formed, whether they know it or not, very young indeed; and *Bevis* shares a quality with *Le Grand Meaulnes*, that of projecting a very different world from the one that is – or was to the middle-class suburban child I had outwardly to be. I cite it as a reminder that the deep pattern, and mood, of such books remains long after one has graduated from them in more obvious ways."

"The lark, the nightingale and Richard Jefferies – those are the three things that brought me to England."

Kate Tryon

LEFT: 'The Fight at the Quarry' – original pencil drawing by E. H. Shepard for the 1932 edition of 'Bevis'.

RIGHT: Woodcut portrait by New York born artist Peter Paul Piech (1920–1996).

BELOW: American artist Kate Tryon (1865–1952).

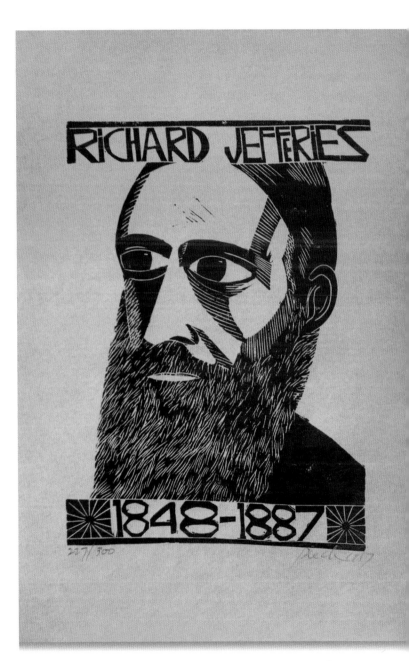

His immense, simple personality is at one with the oak and the grass as if he were somehow involved in their beauty and life. He seems to be conscious of all life that is about him, down to the plants in the arch of a bridge which is lit by reflection from the water.

No other writer leaves us with such a sense of his infinite riches as Jefferies. A book like *Wild Life in a Southern County* seems almost to exhaust a broad strip of English country, and yet it exhausts Jefferies no more than the fields. Hardly a sentence is given to anything but fact. If he did not set everything down, I feel that all Nature was at his right hand.

Yet his big, simple moods will seem to a true lover to enchant his least perfect pages. For he was like the oak tree, which has but three or four moods – when it is bare, when the buds glow, when it is green, when it is ruddy, when it is dead.

These moods are all important to him, and to the tree, and therefore they are beautiful. But the beauty is not always quite human. It is as if he wrote with clay and not with ink. He did not desire the little beauty that is far withdrawing from Nature, and often inspired not so much by its true strangeness as by mere novelty. He would omit nothing by choice. He would seem to have been Nature's advocate, and to have striven to say all. Of course he failed. But his effort is one of the most splendid things recorded in written words, and we have only to read such things as the opening of *My Old Village* to admit that among his other gifts, Nature had given him a great manner, the manner of perfection."

Edward Thomas

A Certain Inheritance

Today, despite his name not having the currency it once did, Jefferies' books are still everywhere, with countless reprints, revised editions, new anthologies and digital versions available at the touch of a button in the age of the Internet. A search on *Richard Jefferies Victorian* will bring back more than a million hits, and every book sales website is brimming with his books.

If you look a little deeper, it turns out Jefferies pops up in other, more unexpected, places; for example, in 2016, his name appears in the opening moments of the BBC's flagship *Proms* programme. To kick off that year's season, the BBC commissioned an original classical piece from composer Julian Anderson. Entitled *Harmony*, the world premiere of the music introduced a haunting choral melody inspired by, and including words from, *The Story of My Heart.* The composer described Jefferies as "one of the most vivid writers on nature and time I've ever come across." Just a couple of years later, streaming movie site Netflix released another, very different premiere: a film called *Annihilation*, starring Hollywood A-lister Natalie Portman. Based on a 2014 science fiction novel from the *Southern Reach* trilogy by American author Jeff VanderMeer, the film depicts a world where mutating plants and animals have appeared and are gradually expanding their territory. In reference to Jefferies, and *After London* particularly, Vandermeer says, "this man was indeed an inspiration while writing the *Southern Reach* trilogy."

These two books, *After London* and *The Story of My Heart*, do seem to elicit more response than other individual works of Jefferies. Will Self's dystopian novel *The Book of Dave* takes us straight back to

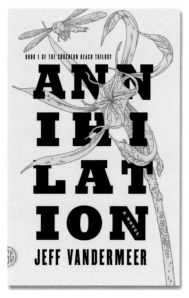 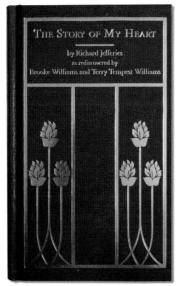

After London, and the author appeared at the University of Greenwich as part of an exhibition based around the book in 2011. Television gardener/writer Monty Don cited *The Story of My Heart* as one of his favourite books on BBC Radio 4's *Open Book.* Of Jefferies himself, Don says: "When we think of the classic idea of the British countryside, people like Thomas Hardy immediately spring to mind, but what Richard Jefferies does is explore the other side of that coin. Jefferies writes about the poverty, the hardship and the injustice of Victorian country life, but at the same time he couples these views with a mystical sense of the immanence of everything, the idea that every leaf, every blade of grass, glows with its own intensity and place in the world."

The Story of My Heart made another appearance in 2014, when American writer, conservationist, and activist, Terry Tempest Williams and her husband Brook discovered an old copy of the book. They immediately fell in love with the work and went on to have it republished with their own thoughts included.

Another citing of the book and another Jefferies 'rediscovery' are discussed in a television programme starring Sir Tony Robinson. In a 2016 edition of *Britain's Ancient Tracks*, Jefferies is credited with the Victorian rediscovery of *The Ridgeway* – the ancient track that runs across the landscape of the South Downs. His recognition of the track's origins and purpose are described in *Wild Life in a Southern County*.

ABOVE: The Royal Albert Hall, London – home of the 'BBC Proms.'

RIGHT: Sir Tony Robinson under the Jefferies mulberry tree during filming for 'Britain's Ancient Tracks.'

LEFT: Covers of Vandermeer's 'Annihilation' and the new edition of ' The Story of My Heart' as rediscovered by the Williams.

215

"The sun is throwing green light on to the paper where I write, through the young leaves of a beech hedge. The air is full of wallflower and lilac smells. A cuckoo repeats itself in the limes on the other side of the house. My feet are wet because the dew is still on the grass and I have slight rheumatism as a result.

If it were not that there are so many books worth mentioning beside me on the table - their binding curling up in the rising heat - I would spend all this column in praise of Richard Jefferies, the great nature writer who was born in the downland country above Swindon."

John Betjeman

217

All That the Earth Bears

Jefferies' most obvious legacy is the abundance of words he produced as a nature writer. His 'celebrity status' may have waned somewhere in the mid-twentieth century – understandably, given changes in literature fashion, styles of writing, and the rise of new media – but the words are still there. Leading ecologist and broadcaster Matthew Oates explains why Jefferies' work is just as relevant now: "Great Nature writers are voices from the past, pointing towards the future. They speak to us, always, from now... Now, as our severance from Nature widens, so Jefferies' messages increase in importance."

Throughout his work Jefferies shares with us the sheer exuberance and scale of nature that he saw everywhere, and constantly interrogates our flawed relationship with it all. In an essay for a re-edition of *Nature Near London,* one of the twenty-first century's great nature writers, Robert Macfarlane, refers to Jefferies' disgust at London's "voracity and greed, and wishing - by means of his writing - to alert the city's inhabitants to the wildlife that existed alongside their own." And as human needs lead to more housing estates, wider motorways, and bigger industrial plants, Jefferies' message goes further, warning us through books like *After London,* that if we ignore it nature can and will fight back.

Such thinking has a lot of resonance with society now. In 2005 *The Guardian* newspaper ran a survey to identify what it described as "the classics of British nature writing." Jefferies received more nominations than any other contender, by far. In the paper's report, also by Macfarlane, Jefferies is described as having "an ability to find the extraordinary in the rurally local." For Macfarlane, "Jefferies located the wild in the strange and ragged interzones of a farmed English landscape – in hedges, ditches, ponds, spinneys – and he wrote about that landscape with... astonishment and wonder."

Another of our great nature writers, Richard Mabey, picked up on that wonder too. In an introduction to a twenty-first century edition of *Wild Life in a Southern County*, Mabey says that the book gave him his first encounter with nature writing, mesmerising him with its "thoughts about how animals might think, and how landscapes made you feel." In describing the qualities of the essays, Mabey sees another warning from the past: "To read these essays today is chastening. There is, in the best of them, an electric attentiveness,

LEFT: Covers of more recent editions of 'Nature Near London' and 'Wild Life in a Southern County'.

a noticing, that is hard to aspire to. They are chastening, too, in what they are able to describe – an abundance of bird and insect life that, despite the contemporary passion for slaughter (in which the author played his part), is unimaginable in the modern industrial countryside. The great set-piece of *Wild Life*, 'Rooks returning to roost' is like an epic Victorian narrative painting, full of intense images – the sound of thousands of black wings 'beating the air with slow steady stroke can hardly be the compared with anything else in its weird oppressiveness'; full too of a sense of the deep history, the natural 'tradition' of these great nightly migrations. And of one stunning statistic: the 'aerial army's line of march extends over quite five miles in one unbroken corps'. Jefferies did not know this, but he was sending, in a faltering new language, a message in a bottle from a disappearing country."

Jefferies' images from the past are also mentioned by John Lewis-Stempel (described by *The Times* as 'Britain's finest living nature writer'): "To get a real picture of a traditional wheat field full of flowers, butterflies, birds and animals, I read the works of the Victorian naturalist, Richard Jefferies. His books gave me a picture from his books of what one could do – actually farm in a way that was full of wildlife, but also quite productive in terms of food for us."

Given Jefferies' impact on today's nature writing, it is perhaps no surprise that the 2019 winner of the Richard Jefferies Society & White Horse Bookshop Literary Prize was Isabella Tree's *Wilding*, and the 2020 winner was Ben Macdonald's *Rebirding*. In response, Macdonald revealed that his relationship with nature writing, like Mabey's, went back to his youth when his wise grandfather gave him a copy of *Wild Life in a Southern County*.

"Another train booms across the iron bridge in the hollow. In a few hours now the carriages will be crowded with men hastening home from their toil in the City. The narrow streak of sunshine which day by day falls for a little while upon the office floor, yellowed by the dingy pane, is all perhaps to remind them of sun and sky, of the forces of nature; and that little is unnoticed. The pressure of business is so severe in these later days, that in the hurry and excitement it is not wonderful many should forget that the world is not comprised in the court of a City thoroughfare... Thus it happens that although the cornfields and the meadows come so closely up to the offices and warehouses of mighty London, there is a line and mark in the minds of man between them; the man of merchandise does not see what the man of the field sees, though both may pass the same acres every morning."

Nature Near London

An Ivy-grown Museum

In E. M. Forster's *Howards End*, the character Leonard believes that writers like Jefferies "mean us to use them for sign-posts, and are not to blame if, in our weakness, we mistake the sign-post for the destination." In his mind there is "something that was greater than Jefferies' books - the spirit that led Jefferies to write them." Jefferies would have agreed with this sentiment. In his last novel, *Amaryllis at the Fair*, he asserts that "no man will ever be able to draw a flying swallow," and reveals himself, the author, in saying that "it is a thousand times more pleasure to me to see a beautiful thing than to write about it. Could I choose I would go on seeing beautiful things, and not writing." Putting his warnings about our ill treatment of the natural world aside, this is something else that Jefferies left us: a reminder to look around; to be astonished and mesmerised by nature; see the beauty that he saw – it may have changed, but it hasn't gone away. It is everywhere.

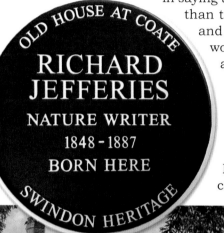

The area where Jefferies grew up, on the edge of Swindon in Wiltshire, does of course have its share of new development, but the hills and fields have not all gone. You can still head off from Jefferies' birthplace at Coate Farm and be surrounded by greenery in just a matter of minutes. Neighbouring Coate Water, where *Bevis* had his adventures, is now a country park designated as a Site of Special Scientific Interest (SSSI).

Jefferies' birthplace, the place he called *the Old House at Coate*, or *Coate Farm*, has not gone away either. Although the fields that used to make up the farmstead have now become part of the country park, and Swindon has grown to reach and even stretch beyond the farm, the original farmhouse, cottage, gardens and some outbuildings remain, in the shadow of the Downs. The site was bought by Swindon Council in 1926 and has been held in public ownership ever since. Today the site is a public museum dedicated to Jefferies and his passions, looked after by a volunteer-run charity – the Richard Jefferies Museum Trust. But it is no ordinary museum (whatever that is); it is not a place for simply admiring a long dead Victorian writer or nodding knowingly at musty volumes of his work; it is not really even about the past. Instead, the museum tries to work on a simple basis of come and enjoy yourselves; do interesting things relating to nature, writing, agriculture, Victorian life; and leave knowing that everything you've experienced was because of a young man called Richard Jefferies.

The museum has plenty of artefacts and books of course, mostly collected by dedicated members of the Richard Jefferies Society, and the site retains much of its original Victorian setting. Over the years it has also put on countless events and activities for every kind of visitor, using the beautiful gardens of the old farm whenever possible. There have been nature rambles, live music performances, children's writing and drawing events, art and craft workshops, theatre shows, vegetable growing, adult writing classes, sculptures, steam engines, toddler groups, poetry recitals, celebrity writer master-classes, fruit picking, chickens, dancers, music classes, reading groups, campfires, puppet shows, school visits, foraging expeditions, art exhibitions, student projects, and the most delicious cream teas! And there have been visitors who have come simply to admire a long dead Victorian writer. They are of course as welcome as everyone else!

Jefferies' home is a place where nature – wild life – is celebrated, in all seasons and all weathers. As well as sharing all the author's works and history, the museum lets visitors learn about the man and his passions through experiencing his world: children play in the same gardens and explore around the same lake as Jefferies; adults dream under the same mulberry tree, in the same natural world. It is the same world where Jefferies dreamt.

LEFT: Blue plaque, and oil painting of the museum as it is today, by Tim Carroll.

RIGHT: The main farmhouse, where Jefferies was born.

224

"*Let us get out of these indoor narrow modern days, whose twelve hours somehow have become shortened, into the sunlight and the pure wind. A something that the ancients thought divine can be found and felt there still.*"

The Amateur Poacher

226

Upwards to a Conclusion

From the start Richard Jefferies was full of conflicts and contradictions, born into rural poverty and sent to live in city society, as his parents grieved over another child. A journalist one day, creative writer the next; his first break was through criticism of farm labourers, but his later works scream at the injustices these same people face. An avid hunter who became a lover of all creatures; cynical of nature's cruelty and mesmerised by her beauty. But this is the wonder of Jefferies. We get the whole picture, all the thoughts and ideas, then all the opposite thoughts and ideas, and some in between. We get his scribbles and mistakes, his dead-ends and lost rambles. He can anger and delight, infuriate and inspire. His works are not written, rewritten, discarded, added to, abandoned, and beaten into perfect shape; in his writing we see the whole person who, like us, is full of doubts and fears, hopes and dreams; we share it all.

Now, all these years later, Jefferies' voice still resonates. He alerts us to our 'civilised' over-exploitation of the natural world, with his descriptions of abundance reminding us of how much has been lost already, and an explicit warning that nature does not care about humanity and will destroy us if we fail to build a better relationship with it. Jefferies believed that humans have an intrinsic beauty, and the capacity to make the necessary changes, but he also believed that it is our greed, profits, selfishness and utter lack of consideration for others that cause the problem, not any shortage of resources in nature. He left us his very own version of mindfulness, reminding us constantly that just *being* in nature, at this moment ("Now is eternity!") is enough to fulfil us. And, through his time spent in nature and his passionate championing of every nook, ditch or tangled thicket, plus everything within them, he advocated the very idea of 'wilding' or 'rewilding' a hundred and seventy five years ago.

Andrew Motion, when Poet Laureate, said "Richard Jefferies is a neglected but indispensable writer; a prose-poet of the English landscape and a pioneer environmentalist." Ecologist Matthew Oates went further, saying that Jefferies was "the most deeply spiritual of our Nature writers and the first and truest nature conservationist." Jefferies suffered many ups and downs in his lifetime, both personally and professionally, but like the wheat as he describes it, he is not going away.

"*It will rise again all the fresher and stronger, for there is something human in wheat, and the more it is trampled on the better it grows. Despots grind half the human race, and despots stronger than man – plague, pestilence, and famine – grind the whole; and yet the world increases, and the green wheat of the human heart is not to be trampled out.*"

Field and Hedgerow

Afterword

Afterword

Deep down, of course, we all know humanity is making a pig's breakfast of it all. We know that nature is suffering and that almost everything we do is to blame. For environmentalists, like me, the challenge is to get people to see this, and then reflect. It is only when people think carefully about how they live that they change. But everyone is too busy going about their business, too focussed on their day-to-day problems, and too numbed by the endlessly gloomy headlines. So they block it all out. The result? Nothing changes.

What is delightful about this book is that it sidesteps all that. It punctures the reader's stupor like a knitting needle shoved between the ribs. The gentle tone of the words and heart-warming photographs ensnare unwittingly. Then, from within the easy-to-digest text comes that powerful thrust to the chest. "Listen!", it shouts. "We must change!"

That is a remarkable feat.

Richard Jefferies was remarkable too. He is one of that very rare breed of ecological writers who is able to tie nature and humanity tightly together, and then throw the clever prose forward, into the future, so that everyone can understand what will happen if we think ourselves too clever for too long.

For more than two centuries, those who live in the rich world have moved ever further from the land, and away from nature. They have lost touch with the soil and the sound of trees. They have lost touch with the wonder that is life, the energy and joy that pulses through the veins of all living things. It is that break with nature which has taken humanity here, to this place, where the push for short-term gain drives progress, and it won't end well.

Jefferies was far ahead of his time. He understood the brutality of the belching machinery which tore through the land (and saw how it tore through the employment registry), the brutality of those who slaughtered innocents dubbed vermin by people who were little different, and the brutality of the system which pushed for the lowest standard because that led to the highest returns.

He didn't get it all right. For years he thought that employees should behave like dutiful slaves, and employers as masters (there were very few women in charge in Victorian England). But he changed his views on that too, when he saw the effects of urbanisation and the workhouses. He realised that social injustice, the greed of a minority and the destruction of nature were all part of the same problem.

Jefferies warned where this will take us. He foresaw the collapse of industrial society, explaining that nature will bite back, and that it will win. Nature doesn't care about us, he said.

Jefferies talked about the language barrier that exists between humans and nature, though today's problem is slightly different. It is not that we are unable to understand the language of the trees suffering from droughts and wildfires, or the voice of the coral dying from higher ocean temperatures and rising acidity. It is that most people don't listen to what is being said because it is too much bother. How can we understand if we don't listen?

We often behave as if there are two worlds: the human world, and the natural world. Yet there is just one, and a close inter-relationship between all living things. Anyone with a heart and common sense can't help but feel love and dismay when they really begin to understand the beauty of nature - love for such a creation, however it came about, and dismay for how it suffers today.

Our relationship with nature is a choice. How we treat the world – and each other – is not determined by some greater intelligence. It is up to us.

In just the same way, humanity is not bound by some otherworldly force to follow the path that currently lies ahead. Humanity has created a difficult future for itself, but it does not need to follow it blindly. Societies can still take a better path, and turn around, if they choose.

Learning from the work of Richard Jefferies, and this book, helps us do that, because he encourages us to stop and listen, to watch and to learn. That's the first step to collective wisdom, and change.

Now is our eternity. Let's live it better.

Graeme Maxton

Graeme Maxton is a British climate change economist and writer. He is an Advisory Board Member of the UN's Energy Pathways Project, and a member of the Editorial Advisory Board of Population Matters.

Bibliography

Jefferies in Print

The following list is necessarily selective. Much of Jefferies' writing was not published in book form in his lifetime and many works, surviving in manuscript or only published in journals, have been published piecemeal by various editors since his death. For a fuller survey, see Miller and Matthews (1993).

Books Published in Jefferies' Lifetime

The Scarlet Shawl (London: Tinsley Brothers, 1874)

Restless Human Hearts (London: Tinsley Brothers, 1875)

World's End (London: Tinsley Brothers, 1877)

The Gamekeeper at Home (London: Smith, Elder & Co., 1878)

Wild Life in a Southern County (London: Smith, Elder & Co., 1879)

The Amateur Poacher (London: Smith, Elder & Co., 1879)

Greene Ferne Farm (London: Smith, Elder & Co., 1880)

Hodge and His Masters (London: Smith, Elder & Co., 1880)

Round About a Great Estate (London: Smith, Elder & Co., 1880)

Wood Magic (London: Cassell, Petter, Galpin & Co., 1881)

Bevis: the Story of a Boy (London: Sampson Low, Marston, Searle, & Rivington, 1882)

Nature Near London (London: Chatto & Windus, 1883)

The Story of My Heart: An Autobiography (London: Longmans, Green, & Co., 1883)

Red Deer (London: Longmans, Green, & Co., 1884)

The Life of the Fields (London: Chatto & Windus, 1884)

The Dewy Morn (London: Richard Bentley and Son, 1884)

After London; Or, Wild England (London: Cassell & Company, Ltd., 1885)

The Open Air (London: Chatto & Windus, 1885)

Amaryllis at the Fair (London: Sampson Low, Marston, Searle, & Rivington, 1887)

Posthumous Publications

Field and Hedgerow; Being the Last Essays of Richard Jefferies (London: Longmans, Green, & Co., 1889)

The Toilers in the Field (London: Longmans, Green, & Co., 1892)

The Early Fiction of Richard Jefferies, ed. G. Toplis (London: Simpkin, Marshall, Hamilton, Kent & Co Ltd., 1896)

Jefferies' Land: A History of Swindon and its Environs, ed. G. Toplis (London: Simpkin, Marshall, Hamilton, Kent & Co Ltd., 1896)

The Hills and the Vale, collected and introduced by E. Thomas (London: Duckworth & Co, 1909)

The Nature Diaries and Notebooks of Richard Jefferies, ed. S. J. Looker (London, Grey Walls Press, 1948)

The Rise of Maximin: Emperor of the Orient, first published in serial form in *The New Monthly Magazine* 1876-7 (Oxfordshire: Petton Books, 2012)

The Farmer's World: Richard Jefferies' Agricultural Journalism in the late 1870s. A collection of Jefferies' articles published in the Livestock Journal. (Norfolk: Petton Books, 2016)

Ben Tubbs Adventures (Norfolk: Petton Books, 2016)

Secondary Literature

R. Arkell, *Richard Jefferies and His Countryside* (Herbert Jenkins, 1946)

J. Banerjee, *Literary Surrey* (John Owen Smith, 2005). pp. 55–56, 64–72

W. Besant, *The Eulogy of Richard Jefferies* (London: Chatto and Windus, 1888)

J. Fowles, Introduction, in R. Jefferies, *After London* (Oxford: OUP, 1980), pp. vii–xxi

W. J. Keith, *Richard Jefferies, A Critical Study* (London: University of Toronto Press, 1965)

Q. D. Leavis, Lives and works of Richard Jefferies, *Scrutiny* 6 (1938) pp. 435-46, reprinted in *Collected Essays* Vol. 3 (Cambridge: Cambridge University Press, 1989), pp. 254–64

S. J. Looker and C. Porteous, *Richard Jefferies, Man of the Fields* (London: John Baker, 1965)

R. Macfarlane, Introduction in *Nature Near London* (London, Collins 2012)

H. Matthews and P. Treitel, *The Forward Life of Richard Jefferies* (Oxfordshire: Petton Books, 1994)

H. Matthews and P. Treitel, *Richard Jefferies: An Index* (Oxfordshire: Petton Books, 2008)

H. Matthews and R. Welshman (eds.), *Richard Jefferies: An Anthology* (Oxfordshire: Petton Books, 2010)

R. Mabey, Introduction in *Wild Life in a Southern County* (Dorset, Little Toller, 2011)

L. W. Mazzeno and R. D. Morrison, Agriculture and ecology in Richard Jefferies' *Hodge and His Masters*, in *Victorian Writers and the Environment* (London & New York, Routledge, 2017) pp. 205-219

G. Miller and H. Matthews, *Richard Jefferies, A bibliographical study* (Aldershot: Scolar Press, 1993)

B. Morris, *Richard Jefferies and the Ecological Vision* (Oxford: Trafford Publishing, 2006)

A. Rossabi (ed.), *Richard Jefferies A Miscellany* (Cambridge, Galileo Publishers, 2019)

A. Rossabi, *(John) Richard Jefferies (1848–1887)*, Oxford Dictionary of National Biography (Oxford: OUP, 2004)

A. Rossabi, *A Peculiarly English Genius, or a Wiltshire Taoist: A Biography of Richard Jefferies, The Early Years, 1848-1867* (Norfolk: Petton Books, 2017)

A. Rossabi, *A Peculiarly English Genius, or a Wiltshire Taoist: A Biography of Richard Jefferies, The Years of Struggle, 1867-1876* (Norfolk: Petton Books, 2020)

A. Smith, *The Interpreter: a biography of Richard Jefferies* (Swindon: Blue Gate Books, 2008)

B. Taylor, *Richard Jefferies* (Boston: Twayne Publishers, 1982)

E. Thomas, *Richard Jefferies: His Life and Work* (London: Hutchinson, 1909)

K. Tryon, *Adventures in the Vale of the White Horse: Jefferies Land* (Oxfordshire: Petton Books, 2010)

H. Sheehan and Jill Carter, *The Cunning Spider* (Swindon: BlueGate Books, 2007)

B. Williams and T. T. Williams, *The Story of My Heart, as rediscovered by Brooke Williams and Terry Tempest Williams* (Salt Lake City, Torrey House Press LLC, 2014)

Credits

Illustration Credits

Objects and old pictures which appear in the book are, unless otherwise indicated, from the collections of the Richard Jefferies Museum, many of them with thanks to the Richard Jefferies Society. All efforts have been made to ensure that other images are used with permission of the creator/owner (directly or via Creative Commons licence), or are recognised as being in the public domain. Copyright remains with the creator/owner. Thanks to all, with special mention of Swindon-based photographers Elmar Rubio, Rob Slade, Rosie Tozer and Phil Messenger, for their generosity and beautiful pictures.

Richard Jefferies Museum
Marlborough Road, Coate
Swindon, Wiltshire SN3 6AA

www.richardjefferies.org